ISBN 0-8373-2394-0

C-2394   CAREER EXAMINATION SERIES

This is your
PASSBOOK® for...

Principal Administrative Associate

Test Preparation Study Guide

Questions & Answers

NATIONAL LEARNING CORPORATION

PASSBOOK®

NOTICE

PASSBOOK SERIES®

THE *PASSBOOK SERIES®* has been created to prepare applicants and candidates for the ultimate academic battlefield – the examination room.

At some time in our lives, each and every one of us may be required to take an examination – for validation, matriculation, admission, qualification, registration, certification, or licensure.

Based on the assumption that every applicant or candidate has met the basic formal educational standards, has taken the required number of courses, and read the necessary texts, the *PASSBOOK SERIES®* furnishes the one special preparation which may assure passing with confidence, instead of failing with insecurity. Examination questions – together with answers – are furnished as the basic vehicle for study so that the mysteries of the examination and its compounding difficulties may be eliminated or diminished by a sure method.

This book is meant to help you pass your examination provided that you qualify and are serious in your objective.

The entire field is reviewed through the huge store of content information which is succinctly presented through a provocative and challenging approach – the question-and-answer method.

A climate of success is established by furnishing the correct answers at the end of each test.

You soon learn to recognize types of questions, forms of questions, and patterns of questioning. You may even begin to anticipate expected outcomes.

You perceive that many questions are repeated or adapted so that you can gain acute insights, which may enable you to score many sure points.

You learn how to confront new questions, or types of questions, and to attack them confidently and work out the correct answers.

You note objectives and emphases, and recognize pitfalls and dangers, so that you may make positive educational adjustments.

Moreover, you are kept fully informed in relation to new concepts, methods, practices, and directions in the field.

You discover that you are actually taking the examination all the time: you are preparing for the examination by "taking" an examination, not by reading extraneous and/or supererogatory textbooks.

In short, this PASSBOOK®, used directedly, should be an important factor in helping you to pass your test.

PRINCIPAL ADMINISTRATIVE ASSOCIATE

DUTIES AND RESPONSIBILITIES

This class of positions encompasses responsible office, supervisory or administrative work of varying degrees of difficulty and with varying degrees of latitude for independent initiative and judgment. There are several assignment levels within this class of positions. The following are typical assignments within this class of positions. All personnel perform related work.

Under general supervision, with some latitude for independent initiative and judgment, performs one of the following difficult and responsible supervisory or administrative functions:

Supervises a large office engaged in routine clerical activities or supervises a small office engaged in departmental, administrative or management activities; or performs difficult and responsible administrative or personnel management work. Supervises a group or section of subordinate personnel in the clerical and related activities performed in an income maintenance center. Performs difficult and responsible administrative work required for the conduct of hearings, control processing, and integrity of dispositions of parking violations; performs related work.

Under general supervision, with considerable latitude for the exercise of independent judgment, makes the necessary arrangements of services and activities in connection with public events, ceremonies, luncheons, and receptions.

Under direction, performs difficult and responsible administrative work in the capacity of Secretary to a very high level executive.

Under direction, with considerable latitude for independent action or decision, performs difficult and responsible supervisory or administrative work in any one or more of the following:

Administers all matters pertaining to the general municipal telephone system. Supervises a very large office engaged in routine clerical or personnel management work.

Under general direction and with wide latitude for the exercise of independent initiative and judgment performs the following:

Supervises an exceptionally large office engaged in routine clerical activities, or supervises a very large office engaged in departmental administrative or management activities. Performs exceptionally difficult and responsible independent, specialized administrative or management work related to accounts and budgeting, methods and organization, etc. Plans, directs and supervises a minimal personnel management program covering a large number of employees, or a well-developed personnel management program including several major personnel activities covering a moderate number of employees or performs appropriate professional duties in a personnel program headed by an employee of higher rank.

TESTS

The written test will be of the multiple-choice type and may include questions on supervision and administration; reading comprehension and English usage; judgment in job situations; human relations; personnel management; and other related areas.

———

HOW TO TAKE A TEST

I. YOU MUST PASS AN EXAMINATION

A. *WHAT EVERY CANDIDATE SHOULD KNOW*

Examination applicants often ask us for help in preparing for the written test. What can I study in advance? What kinds of questions will be asked? How will the test be given? How will the papers be graded?

As an applicant for a civil service examination, you may be wondering about some of these things. Our purpose here is to suggest effective methods of advance study and to describe civil service examinations.

Your chances for success on this examination can be increased if you know how to prepare. Those "pre-examination jitters" can be reduced if you know what to expect. You can even experience an adventure in good citizenship if you know why civil service exams are given.

B. *WHY ARE CIVIL SERVICE EXAMINATIONS GIVEN?*

Civil service examinations are important to you in two ways. As a citizen, you want public jobs filled by employees who know how to do their work. As a job seeker, you want a fair chance to compete for that job on an equal footing with other candidates. The best-known means of accomplishing this two-fold goal is the competitive examination.

Exams are widely publicized throughout the nation. They may be administered for jobs in federal, state, city, municipal, town or village governments or agencies.

Any citizen may apply, with some limitations, such as the age or residence of applicants. Your experience and education may be reviewed to see whether you meet the requirements for the particular examination. When these requirements exist, they are reasonable and applied consistently to all applicants. Thus, a competitive examination may cause you some uneasiness now, but it is your privilege and safeguard.

C. *HOW ARE CIVIL SERVICE EXAMS DEVELOPED?*

Examinations are carefully written by trained technicians who are specialists in the field known as "psychological measurement," in consultation with recognized authorities in the field of work that the test will cover. These experts recommend the subject matter areas or skills to be tested; only those knowledges or skills important to your success on the job are included. The most reliable books and source materials available are used as references. Together, the experts and technicians judge the difficulty level of the questions.

Test technicians know how to phrase questions so that the problem is clearly stated. Their ethics do not permit "trick" or "catch" questions. Questions may have been tried out on sample groups, or subjected to statistical analysis, to determine their usefulness.

Written tests are often used in combination with performance tests, ratings of training and experience, and oral interviews. All of these measures combine to form the best-known means of finding the right person for the right job.

II. HOW TO PASS THE WRITTEN TEST

A. NATURE OF THE EXAMINATION

To prepare intelligently for civil service examinations, you should know how they differ from school examinations you have taken. In school you were assigned certain definite pages to read or subjects to cover. The examination questions were quite detailed and usually emphasized memory. Civil service exams, on the other hand, try to discover your present ability to perform the duties of a position, plus your potentiality to learn these duties. In other words, a civil service exam attempts to predict how successful you will be. Questions cover such a broad area that they cannot be as minute and detailed as school exam questions.

In the public service similar kinds of work, or positions, are grouped together in one "class." This process is known as *position-classification*. All the positions in a class are paid according to the salary range for that class. One class title covers all of these positions, and they are all tested by the same examination.

B. FOUR BASIC STEPS

1) Study the announcement

How, then, can you know what subjects to study? Our best answer is: "Learn as much as possible about the class of positions for which you've applied." The exam will test the knowledge, skills and abilities needed to do the work.

Your most valuable source of information about the position you want is the official exam announcement. This announcement lists the training and experience qualifications. Check these standards and apply only if you come reasonably close to meeting them.

The brief description of the position in the examination announcement offers some clues to the subjects which will be tested. Think about the job itself. Review the duties in your mind. Can you perform them, or are there some in which you are rusty? Fill in the blank spots in your preparation.

Many jurisdictions preview the written test in the exam announcement by including a section called "Knowledge and Abilities Required," "Scope of the Examination," or some similar heading. Here you will find out specifically what fields will be tested.

2) Review your own background

Once you learn in general what the position is all about, and what you need to know to do the work, ask yourself which subjects you already know fairly well and which need improvement. You may wonder whether to concentrate on improving your strong areas or on building some background in your fields of weakness. When the announcement has specified "some knowledge" or "considerable knowledge," or has used adjectives like "beginning principles of…" or "advanced … methods," you can get a clue as to the number and difficulty of questions to be asked in any given field. More questions, and hence broader coverage, would be included for those subjects which are more important in the work. Now weigh your strengths and weaknesses against the job requirements and prepare accordingly.

3) Determine the level of the position

Another way to tell how intensively you should prepare is to understand the level of the job for which you are applying. Is it the entering level? In other words, is this the position in which beginners in a field of work are hired? Or is it an intermediate or advanced level? Sometimes this is indicated by such words as "Junior" or "Senior" in the class title. Other jurisdictions use Roman numerals to designate the level – Clerk I, Clerk II, for example. The word "Supervisor" sometimes appears in the title. If the level is not indicated by the title, check the description of duties. Will you be working under very close supervision, or will you have responsibility for independent decisions in this work?

4) Choose appropriate study materials

Now that you know the subjects to be examined and the relative amount of each subject to be covered, you can choose suitable study materials. For beginning level jobs, or even advanced ones, if you have a pronounced weakness in some aspect of your training, read a modern, standard textbook in that field. Be sure it is up to date and has general coverage. Such books are normally available at your library, and the librarian will be glad to help you locate one. For entry-level positions, questions of appropriate difficulty are chosen – neither highly advanced questions, nor those too simple. Such questions require careful thought but not advanced training.

If the position for which you are applying is technical or advanced, you will read more advanced, specialized material. If you are already familiar with the basic principles of your field, elementary textbooks would waste your time. Concentrate on advanced textbooks and technical periodicals. Think through the concepts and review difficult problems in your field.

These are all general sources. You can get more ideas on your own initiative, following these leads. For example, training manuals and publications of the government agency which employs workers in your field can be useful, particularly for technical and professional positions. A letter or visit to the government department involved may result in more specific study suggestions, and certainly will provide you with a more definite idea of the exact nature of the position you are seeking.

III. KINDS OF TESTS

Tests are used for purposes other than measuring knowledge and ability to perform specified duties. For some positions, it is equally important to test ability to make adjustments to new situations or to profit from training. In others, basic mental abilities not dependent on information are essential. Questions which test these things may not appear as pertinent to the duties of the position as those which test for knowledge and information. Yet they are often highly important parts of a fair examination. For very general questions, it is almost impossible to help you direct your study efforts. What we can do is to point out some of the more common of these general abilities needed in public service positions and describe some typical questions.

1) General information

Broad, general information has been found useful for predicting job success in some kinds of work. This is tested in a variety of ways, from vocabulary lists to questions about current events. Basic background in some field of work, such as sociology or economics, may be sampled in a group of questions. Often these are principles which have become familiar to most persons through exposure rather than through formal training. It is difficult to advise you how to study for these questions; being alert to the world around you is our best suggestion.

2) Verbal ability

An example of an ability needed in many positions is verbal or language ability. Verbal ability is, in brief, the ability to use and understand words. Vocabulary and grammar tests are typical measures of this ability. Reading comprehension or paragraph interpretation questions are common in many kinds of civil service tests. You are given a paragraph of written material and asked to find its central meaning.

3) Numerical ability

Number skills can be tested by the familiar arithmetic problem, by checking paired lists of numbers to see which are alike and which are different, or by interpreting charts and graphs. In the latter test, a graph may be printed in the test booklet which you are asked to use as the basis for answering questions.

4) Observation

A popular test for law-enforcement positions is the observation test. A picture is shown to you for several minutes, then taken away. Questions about the picture test your ability to observe both details and larger elements.

5) Following directions

In many positions in the public service, the employee must be able to carry out written instructions dependably and accurately. You may be given a chart with several columns, each column listing a variety of information. The questions require you to carry out directions involving the information given in the chart.

6) Skills and aptitudes

Performance tests effectively measure some manual skills and aptitudes. When the skill is one in which you are trained, such as typing or shorthand, you can practice. These tests are often very much like those given in business school or high school courses. For many of the other skills and aptitudes, however, no short-time preparation can be made. Skills and abilities natural to you or that you have developed throughout your lifetime are being tested.

Many of the general questions just described provide all the data needed to answer the questions and ask you to use your reasoning ability to find the answers. Your best preparation for these tests, as well as for tests of facts and ideas, is to be at your physical and mental best. You, no doubt, have your own methods of getting into an exam-taking mood and keeping "in shape." The next section lists some ideas on this subject.

IV. KINDS OF QUESTIONS

Only rarely is the "essay" question, which you answer in narrative form, used in civil service tests. Civil service tests are usually of the short-answer type. Full instructions for answering these questions will be given to you at the examination. But in case this is your first experience with short-answer questions and separate answer sheets, here is what you need to know:

1) Multiple-choice Questions

Most popular of the short-answer questions is the "multiple choice" or "best answer" question. It can be used, for example, to test for factual knowledge, ability to solve problems or judgment in meeting situations found at work.

A multiple-choice question is normally one of three types—

- It can begin with an incomplete statement followed by several possible endings. You are to find the one ending which *best* completes the statement, although some of the others may not be entirely wrong.
- It can also be a complete statement in the form of a question which is answered by choosing one of the statements listed.
- It can be in the form of a problem – again you select the best answer.

Here is an example of a multiple-choice question with a discussion which should give you some clues as to the method for choosing the right answer:

When an employee has a complaint about his assignment, the action which will *best* help him overcome his difficulty is to
- A. discuss his difficulty with his coworkers
- B. take the problem to the head of the organization
- C. take the problem to the person who gave him the assignment
- D. say nothing to anyone about his complaint

In answering this question, you should study each of the choices to find which is best. Consider choice "A" – Certainly an employee may discuss his complaint with fellow employees, but no change or improvement can result, and the complaint remains unresolved. Choice "B" is a poor choice since the head of the organization probably does not know what assignment you have been given, and taking your problem to him is known as "going over the head" of the supervisor. The supervisor, or person who made the assignment, is the person who can clarify it or correct any injustice. Choice "C" is, therefore, correct. To say nothing, as in choice "D," is unwise. Supervisors have and interest in knowing the problems employees are facing, and the employee is seeking a solution to his problem.

2) True/False Questions

The "true/false" or "right/wrong" form of question is sometimes used. Here a complete statement is given. Your job is to decide whether the statement is right or wrong.

SAMPLE: A person-to-person long-distance telephone call costs less than a station-to-station call to the same city.

This statement is wrong, or false, since person-to-person calls are more expensive.

This is not a complete list of all possible question forms, although most of the others are variations of these common types. You will always get complete directions for answering questions. Be sure you understand *how* to mark your answers – ask questions until you do.

V. RECORDING YOUR ANSWERS

For an examination with very few applicants, you may be told to record your answers in the test booklet itself. Separate answer sheets are much more common. If this separate answer sheet is to be scored by machine – and this is often the case – it is highly important that you mark your answers correctly in order to get credit.

An electric scoring machine is often used in civil service offices because of the speed with which papers can be scored. Machine-scored answer sheets must be marked with a pencil, which will be given to you. This pencil has a high graphite content which responds to the electric scoring machine. As a matter of fact, stray dots may register as answers, so do not let your pencil rest on the answer sheet while you are pondering the correct answer. Also, if your pencil lead breaks or is otherwise defective, ask for another.

Since the answer sheet will be dropped in a slot in the scoring machine, be careful not to bend the corners or get the paper crumpled.

The answer sheet normally has five vertical columns of numbers, with 30 numbers to a column. These numbers correspond to the question numbers in your test booklet. After each number, going across the page are four or five pairs of dotted lines. These short dotted lines have small letters or numbers above them. The first two pairs may also have a "T" or "F" above the letters. This indicates that the first two pairs only are to be used if the questions are of the true-false type. If the questions are multiple choice, disregard the "T" and "F" and pay attention only to the small letters or numbers.

Answer your questions in the manner of the sample that follows:

32. The largest city in the United States is
    A. Washington, D.C.
    B. New York City
    C. Chicago
    D. Detroit
    E. San Francisco

1) Choose the answer you think is best. (New York City is the largest, so "B" is correct.)
2) Find the row of dotted lines numbered the same as the question you are answering. (Find row number 32)
3) Find the pair of dotted lines corresponding to the answer. (Find the pair of lines under the mark "B.")
4) Make a solid black mark between the dotted lines.

VI. BEFORE THE TEST

Common sense will help you find procedures to follow to get ready for an examination. Too many of us, however, overlook these sensible measures. Indeed, nervousness and fatigue have been found to be the most serious reasons why applicants fail to do their best on civil service tests. Here is a list of reminders:

- Begin your preparation early – Don't wait until the last minute to go scurrying around for books and materials or to find out what the position is all about.
- Prepare continuously – An hour a night for a week is better than an all-night cram session. This has been definitely established. What is more, a night a

week for a month will return better dividends than crowding your study into a shorter period of time.

- Locate the place of the exam – You have been sent a notice telling you when and where to report for the examination. If the location is in a different town or otherwise unfamiliar to you, it would be well to inquire the best route and learn something about the building.
- Relax the night before the test – Allow your mind to rest. Do not study at all that night. Plan some mild recreation or diversion; then go to bed early and get a good night's sleep.
- Get up early enough to make a leisurely trip to the place for the test – This way unforeseen events, traffic snarls, unfamiliar buildings, etc. will not upset you.
- Dress comfortably – A written test is not a fashion show. You will be known by number and not by name, so wear something comfortable.
- Leave excess paraphernalia at home – Shopping bags and odd bundles will get in your way. You need bring only the items mentioned in the official notice you received; usually everything you need is provided. Do not bring reference books to the exam. They will only confuse those last minutes and be taken away from you when in the test room.
- Arrive somewhat ahead of time – If because of transportation schedules you must get there very early, bring a newspaper or magazine to take your mind off yourself while waiting.
- Locate the examination room – When you have found the proper room, you will be directed to the seat or part of the room where you will sit. Sometimes you are given a sheet of instructions to read while you are waiting. Do not fill out any forms until you are told to do so; just read them and be prepared.
- Relax and prepare to listen to the instructions
- If you have any physical problem that may keep you from doing your best, be sure to tell the test administrator. If you are sick or in poor health, you really cannot do your best on the exam. You can come back and take the test some other time.

VII. AT THE TEST

The day of the test is here and you have the test booklet in your hand. The temptation to get going is very strong. Caution! There is more to success than knowing the right answers. You must know how to identify your papers and understand variations in the type of short-answer question used in this particular examination. Follow these suggestions for maximum results from your efforts:

1) Cooperate with the monitor

The test administrator has a duty to create a situation in which you can be as much at ease as possible. He will give instructions, tell you when to begin, check to see that you are marking your answer sheet correctly, and so on. He is not there to guard you, although he will see that your competitors do not take unfair advantage. He wants to help you do your best.

2) Listen to all instructions

Don't jump the gun! Wait until you understand all directions. In most civil service tests you get more time than you need to answer the questions. So don't be in a hurry.

Read each word of instructions until you clearly understand the meaning. Study the examples, listen to all announcements and follow directions. Ask questions if you do not understand what to do.

3) Identify your papers

Civil service exams are usually identified by number only. You will be assigned a number; you must not put your name on your test papers. Be sure to copy your number correctly. Since more than one exam may be given, copy your exact examination title.

4) Plan your time

Unless you are told that a test is a "speed" or "rate of work" test, speed itself is usually not important. Time enough to answer all the questions will be provided, but this does not mean that you have all day. An overall time limit has been set. Divide the total time (in minutes) by the number of questions to determine the approximate time you have for each question.

5) Do not linger over difficult questions

If you come across a difficult question, mark it with a paper clip (useful to have along) and come back to it when you have been through the booklet. One caution if you do this – be sure to skip a number on your answer sheet as well. Check often to be sure that you have not lost your place and that you are marking in the row numbered the same as the question you are answering.

6) Read the questions

Be sure you know what the question asks! Many capable people are unsuccessful because they failed to *read* the questions correctly.

7) Answer all questions

Unless you have been instructed that a penalty will be deducted for incorrect answers, it is better to guess than to omit a question.

8) Speed tests

It is often better NOT to guess on speed tests. It has been found that on timed tests people are tempted to spend the last few seconds before time is called in marking answers at random – without even reading them – in the hope of picking up a few extra points. To discourage this practice, the instructions may warn you that your score will be "corrected" for guessing. That is, a penalty will be applied. The incorrect answers will be deducted from the correct ones, or some other penalty formula will be used.

9) Review your answers

If you finish before time is called, go back to the questions you guessed or omitted to give them further thought. Review other answers if you have time.

10) Return your test materials

If you are ready to leave before others have finished or time is called, take ALL your materials to the monitor and leave quietly. Never take any test material with you. The monitor can discover whose papers are not complete, and taking a test booklet may be grounds for disqualification.

VIII. EXAMINATION TECHNIQUES

1) Read the general instructions carefully. These are usually printed on the first page of the exam booklet. As a rule, these instructions refer to the timing of the examination; the fact that you should not start work until the signal and must stop work at a signal, etc. If there are any *special* instructions, such as a choice of questions to be answered, make sure that you note this instruction carefully.

2) When you are ready to start work on the examination, that is as soon as the signal has been given, read the instructions to each question booklet, underline any key words or phrases, such as *least, best, outline, describe* and the like. In this way you will tend to answer as requested rather than discover on reviewing your paper that you *listed without describing*, that you selected the *worst* choice rather than the *best* choice, etc.

3) If the examination is of the objective or multiple-choice type – that is, each question will also give a series of possible answers: A, B, C or D, and you are called upon to select the best answer and write the letter next to that answer on your answer paper – it is advisable to start answering each question in turn. There may be anywhere from 50 to 100 such questions in the three or four hours allotted and you can see how much time would be taken if you read through all the questions before beginning to answer any. Furthermore, if you come across a question or group of questions which you know would be difficult to answer, it would undoubtedly affect your handling of all the other questions.

4) If the examination is of the essay type and contains but a few questions, it is a moot point as to whether you should read all the questions before starting to answer any one. Of course, if you are given a choice – say five out of seven and the like – then it is essential to read all the questions so you can eliminate the two that are most difficult. If, however, you are asked to answer all the questions, there may be danger in trying to answer the easiest one first because you may find that you will spend too much time on it. The best technique is to answer the first question, then proceed to the second, etc.

5) Time your answers. Before the exam begins, write down the time it started, then add the time allowed for the examination and write down the time it must be completed, then divide the time available somewhat as follows:
   - If 3-1/2 hours are allowed, that would be 210 minutes. If you have 80 objective-type questions, that would be an average of 2-1/2 minutes per question. Allow yourself no more than 2 minutes per question, or a total of 160 minutes, which will permit about 50 minutes to review.
   - If for the time allotment of 210 minutes there are 7 essay questions to answer, that would average about 30 minutes a question. Give yourself only 25 minutes per question so that you have about 35 minutes to review.

6) The most important instruction is to *read each question* and make sure you know what is wanted. The second most important instruction is to *time yourself properly* so that you answer every question. The third most

important instruction is to *answer every question.* Guess if you have to but include something for each question. Remember that you will receive no credit for a blank and will probably receive some credit if you write something in answer to an essay question. If you guess a letter – say "B" for a multiple-choice question – you may have guessed right. If you leave a blank as an answer to a multiple-choice question, the examiners may respect your feelings but it will not add a point to your score. Some exams may penalize you for wrong answers, so in such cases *only,* you may not want to guess unless you have some basis for your answer.

7) Suggestions
    a. Objective-type questions
        1. Examine the question booklet for proper sequence of pages and questions
        2. Read all instructions carefully
        3. Skip any question which seems too difficult; return to it after all other questions have been answered
        4. Apportion your time properly; do not spend too much time on any single question or group of questions
        5. Note and underline key words – *all, most, fewest, least, best, worst, same, opposite,* etc.
        6. Pay particular attention to negatives
        7. Note unusual option, e.g., unduly long, short, complex, different or similar in content to the body of the question
        8. Observe the use of "hedging" words – *probably, may, most likely,* etc.
        9. Make sure that your answer is put next to the same number as the question
        10. Do not second-guess unless you have good reason to believe the second answer is definitely more correct
        11. Cross out original answer if you decide another answer is more accurate; do not erase until you are ready to hand your paper in
        12. Answer all questions; guess unless instructed otherwise
        13. Leave time for review

    b. Essay questions
        1. Read each question carefully
        2. Determine exactly what is wanted. Underline key words or phrases.
        3. Decide on outline or paragraph answer
        4. Include many different points and elements unless asked to develop any one or two points or elements
        5. Show impartiality by giving pros and cons unless directed to select one side only
        6. Make and write down any assumptions you find necessary to answer the questions
        7. Watch your English, grammar, punctuation and choice of words
        8. Time your answers; don't crowd material

8) Answering the essay question

Most essay questions can be answered by framing the specific response around several key words or ideas. Here are a few such key words or ideas:

M's: manpower, materials, methods, money, management

P's: purpose, program, policy, plan, procedure, practice, problems, pitfalls, personnel, public relations

    a. Six basic steps in handling problems:

        1. Preliminary plan and background development
        2. Collect information, data and facts
        3. Analyze and interpret information, data and facts
        4. Analyze and develop solutions as well as make recommendations
        5. Prepare report and sell recommendations
        6. Install recommendations and follow up effectiveness

    b. Pitfalls to avoid

        1. *Taking things for granted* – A statement of the situation does not necessarily imply that each of the elements is necessarily true; for example, a complaint may be invalid and biased so that all that can be taken for granted is that a complaint has been registered
        2. *Considering only one side of a situation* – Wherever possible, indicate several alternatives and then point out the reasons you selected the best one
        3. *Failing to indicate follow up* – Whenever your answer indicates action on your part, make certain that you will take proper follow-up action to see how successful your recommendations, procedures or actions turn out to be
        4. *Taking too long in answering any single question* – Remember to time your answers properly

IX. AFTER THE TEST

Scoring procedures differ in detail among civil service jurisdictions although the general principles are the same. Whether the papers are hand-scored or graded by machine we have described, they are nearly always graded by number. That is, the person who marks the paper knows only the number – never the name – of the applicant. Not until all the papers have been graded will they be matched with names. If other tests, such as training and experience or oral interview ratings have been given, scores will be combined. Different parts of the examination usually have different weights. For example, the written test might count 60 percent of the final grade, and a rating of training and experience 40 percent. In many jurisdictions, veterans will have a certain number of points added to their grades.

After the final grade has been determined, the names are placed in grade order and an eligible list is established. There are various methods for resolving ties between those who get the same final grade – probably the most common is to place first the name of the person whose application was received first. Job offers are made from the eligible list in the order the names appear on it. You will be notified of your grade and your rank as soon as all these computations have been made. This will be done as rapidly as possible.

People who are found to meet the requirements in the announcement are called "eligibles." Their names are put on a list of eligible candidates. An eligible's chances of getting a job depend on how high he stands on this list and how fast agencies are filling jobs from the list.

When a job is to be filled from a list of eligibles, the agency asks for the names of people on the list of eligibles for that job. When the civil service commission receives this request, it sends to the agency the names of the three people highest on this list. Or, if the job to be filled has specialized requirements, the office sends the agency the names of the top three persons who meet these requirements from the general list.

The appointing officer makes a choice from among the three people whose names were sent to him. If the selected person accepts the appointment, the names of the others are put back on the list to be considered for future openings.

That is the rule in hiring from all kinds of eligible lists, whether they are for typist, carpenter, chemist, or something else. For every vacancy, the appointing officer has his choice of any one of the top three eligibles on the list. This explains why the person whose name is on top of the list sometimes does not get an appointment when some of the persons lower on the list do. If the appointing officer chooses the second or third eligible, the No. 1 eligible does not get a job at once, but stays on the list until he is appointed or the list is terminated.

X. HOW TO PASS THE INTERVIEW TEST

The examination for which you applied requires an oral interview test. You have already taken the written test and you are now being called for the interview test – the final part of the formal examination.

You may think that it is not possible to prepare for an interview test and that there are no procedures to follow during an interview. Our purpose is to point out some things you can do in advance that will help you and some good rules to follow and pitfalls to avoid while you are being interviewed.

What is an interview supposed to test?

The written examination is designed to test the technical knowledge and competence of the candidate; the oral is designed to evaluate intangible qualities, not readily measured otherwise, and to establish a list showing the relative fitness of each candidate – as measured against his competitors – for the position sought. Scoring is not on the basis of "right" and "wrong," but on a sliding scale of values ranging from "not passable" to "outstanding." As a matter of fact, it is possible to achieve a relatively low score without a single "incorrect" answer because of evident weakness in the qualities being measured.

Occasionally, an examination may consist entirely of an oral test – either an individual or a group oral. In such cases, information is sought concerning the technical knowledges and abilities of the candidate, since there has been no written examination for this purpose. More commonly, however, an oral test is used to supplement a written examination.

Who conducts interviews?

The composition of oral boards varies among different jurisdictions. In nearly all, a representative of the personnel department serves as chairman. One of the members of the board may be a representative of the department in which the candidate would work. In some cases, "outside experts" are used, and, frequently, a businessman or some other representative of the general public is asked to serve. Labor and management or other special groups may be represented. The aim is to secure the services of experts in the appropriate field.

However the board is composed, it is a good idea (and not at all improper or unethical) to ascertain in advance of the interview who the members are and what groups they represent. When you are introduced to them, you will have some idea of their backgrounds and interests, and at least you will not stutter and stammer over their names.

What should be done before the interview?

While knowledge about the board members is useful and takes some of the surprise element out of the interview, there is other preparation which is more substantive. It *is* possible to prepare for an oral interview – in several ways:

1) Keep a copy of your application and review it carefully before the interview

This may be the only document before the oral board, and the starting point of the interview. Know what education and experience you have listed there, and the sequence and dates of all of it. Sometimes the board will ask you to review the highlights of your experience for them; you should not have to hem and haw doing it.

2) Study the class specification and the examination announcement

Usually, the oral board has one or both of these to guide them. The qualities, characteristics or knowledges required by the position sought are stated in these documents. They offer valuable clues as to the nature of the oral interview. For example, if the job involves supervisory responsibilities, the announcement will usually indicate that knowledge of modern supervisory methods and the qualifications of the candidate as a supervisor will be tested. If so, you can expect such questions, frequently in the form of a hypothetical situation which you are expected to solve. NEVER go into an oral without knowledge of the duties and responsibilities of the job you seek.

3) Think through each qualification required

Try to visualize the kind of questions you would ask if you were a board member. How well could you answer them? Try especially to appraise your own knowledge and background in each area, *measured against the job sought*, and identify any areas in which you are weak. Be critical and realistic – do not flatter yourself.

4) Do some general reading in areas in which you feel you may be weak

For example, if the job involves supervision and your past experience has NOT, some general reading in supervisory methods and practices, particularly in the field of human relations, might be useful. Do NOT study agency procedures or detailed manuals. The oral board will be testing your understanding and capacity, not your memory.

5) Get a good night's sleep and watch your general health and mental attitude

You will want a clear head at the interview. Take care of a cold or any other minor ailment, and of course, no hangovers.

What should be done on the day of the interview?

Now comes the day of the interview itself. Give yourself plenty of time to get there. Plan to arrive somewhat ahead of the scheduled time, particularly if your appointment is in the fore part of the day. If a previous candidate fails to appear, the board might be ready for you a bit early. By early afternoon an oral board is almost invariably behind schedule if there are many candidates, and you may have to wait.

Take along a book or magazine to read, or your application to review, but leave any extraneous material in the waiting room when you go in for your interview. In any event, relax and compose yourself.

The matter of dress is important. The board is forming impressions about you – from your experience, your manners, your attitude, and your appearance. Give your personal appearance careful attention. Dress your best, but not your flashiest. Choose conservative, appropriate clothing, and be sure it is immaculate. This is a business interview, and your appearance should indicate that you regard it as such. Besides, being well groomed and properly dressed will help boost your confidence.

Sooner or later, someone will call your name and escort you into the interview room. *This is it.* From here on you are on your own. It is too late for any more preparation. But remember, you asked for this opportunity to prove your fitness, and you are here because your request was granted.

What happens when you go in?

The usual sequence of events will be as follows: The clerk (who is often the board stenographer) will introduce you to the chairman of the oral board, who will introduce you to the other members of the board. Acknowledge the introductions before you sit down. Do not be surprised if you find a microphone facing you or a stenotypist sitting by. Oral interviews are usually recorded in the event of an appeal or other review.

Usually the chairman of the board will open the interview by reviewing the highlights of your education and work experience from your application – primarily for the benefit of the other members of the board, as well as to get the material into the record. Do not interrupt or comment unless there is an error or significant misinterpretation; if that is the case, do not hesitate. But do not quibble about insignificant matters. Also, he will usually ask you some question about your education, experience or your present job – partly to get you to start talking and to establish the interviewing "rapport." He may start the actual questioning, or turn it over to one of the other members. Frequently, each member undertakes the questioning on a particular area, one in which he is perhaps most competent, so you can expect each member to participate in the examination. Because time is limited, you may also expect some rather abrupt switches in the direction the questioning takes, so do not be upset by it. Normally, a board member will not pursue a single line of questioning unless he discovers a particular strength or weakness.

After each member has participated, the chairman will usually ask whether any member has any further questions, then will ask you if you have anything you wish to add. Unless you are expecting this question, it may floor you. Worse, it may start you off on an extended, extemporaneous speech. The board is not usually seeking more information. The question is principally to offer you a last opportunity to present further qualifications or to indicate that you have nothing to add. So, if you feel that a significant qualification or characteristic has been overlooked, it is proper to point it out in a sentence or so. Do not compliment the board on the thoroughness of their examination – they have been sketchy, and you know it. If you wish, merely say, "No thank you, I have nothing further to add." This is a point where you can "talk yourself out" of a good impression or fail to present an important bit of information. Remember, *you close the interview yourself.*

The chairman will then say, "That is all, Mr. _____, thank you." Do not be startled; the interview is over, and quicker than you think. Thank him, gather your belongings and take your leave. Save your sigh of relief for the other side of the door.

How to put your best foot forward

Throughout this entire process, you may feel that the board individually and collectively is trying to pierce your defenses, seek out your hidden weaknesses and embarrass and confuse you. Actually, this is not true. They are obliged to make an appraisal of your qualifications for the job you are seeking, and they want to see you in your best light. Remember, they must interview all candidates and a non-cooperative candidate may become a failure in spite of their best efforts to bring out his qualifications. Here are 15 suggestions that will help you:

1) Be natural – Keep your attitude confident, not cocky

If you are not confident that you can do the job, do not expect the board to be. Do not apologize for your weaknesses, try to bring out your strong points. The board is interested in a positive, not negative, presentation. Cockiness will antagonize any board member and make him wonder if you are covering up a weakness by a false show of strength.

2) Get comfortable, but don't lounge or sprawl

Sit erectly but not stiffly. A careless posture may lead the board to conclude that you are careless in other things, or at least that you are not impressed by the importance of the occasion. Either conclusion is natural, even if incorrect. Do not fuss with your clothing, a pencil or an ashtray. Your hands may occasionally be useful to emphasize a point; do not let them become a point of distraction.

3) Do not wisecrack or make small talk

This is a serious situation, and your attitude should show that you consider it as such. Further, the time of the board is limited – they do not want to waste it, and neither should you.

4) Do not exaggerate your experience or abilities

In the first place, from information in the application or other interviews and sources, the board may know more about you than you think. Secondly, you probably will not get away with it. An experienced board is rather adept at spotting such a situation, so do not take the chance.

5) If you know a board member, do not make a point of it, yet do not hide it

Certainly you are not fooling him, and probably not the other members of the board. Do not try to take advantage of your acquaintanceship – it will probably do you little good.

6) Do not dominate the interview

Let the board do that. They will give you the clues – do not assume that you have to do all the talking. Realize that the board has a number of questions to ask you, and do not try to take up all the interview time by showing off your extensive knowledge of the answer to the first one.

7) Be attentive

You only have 20 minutes or so, and you should keep your attention at its sharpest throughout. When a member is addressing a problem or question to you, give him your undivided attention. Address your reply principally to him, but do not exclude the other board members.

8) Do not interrupt

A board member may be stating a problem for you to analyze. He will ask you a question when the time comes. Let him state the problem, and wait for the question.

9) Make sure you understand the question

Do not try to answer until you are sure what the question is. If it is not clear, restate it in your own words or ask the board member to clarify it for you. However, do not haggle about minor elements.

10) Reply promptly but not hastily

A common entry on oral board rating sheets is "candidate responded readily," or "candidate hesitated in replies." Respond as promptly and quickly as you can, but do not jump to a hasty, ill-considered answer.

11) Do not be peremptory in your answers

A brief answer is proper – but do not fire your answer back. That is a losing game from your point of view. The board member can probably ask questions much faster than you can answer them.

12) Do not try to create the answer you think the board member wants

He is interested in what kind of mind you have and how it works – not in playing games. Furthermore, he can usually spot this practice and will actually grade you down on it.

13) Do not switch sides in your reply merely to agree with a board member

Frequently, a member will take a contrary position merely to draw you out and to see if you are willing and able to defend your point of view. Do not start a debate, yet do not surrender a good position. If a position is worth taking, it is worth defending.

14) Do not be afraid to admit an error in judgment if you are shown to be wrong

The board knows that you are forced to reply without any opportunity for careful consideration. Your answer may be demonstrably wrong. If so, admit it and get on with the interview.

15) Do not dwell at length on your present job

The opening question may relate to your present assignment. Answer the question but do not go into an extended discussion. You are being examined for a *new* job, not your present one. As a matter of fact, try to phrase ALL your answers in terms of the job for which you are being examined.

Basis of Rating

Probably you will forget most of these "do's" and "don'ts" when you walk into the oral interview room. Even remembering them all will not ensure you a passing grade. Perhaps you did not have the qualifications in the first place. But remembering them will help you to put your best foot forward, without treading on the toes of the board members.

Rumor and popular opinion to the contrary notwithstanding, an oral board wants you to make the best appearance possible. They know you are under pressure – but they also want to see how you respond to it as a guide to what your reaction would be under the pressures of the job you seek. They will be influenced by the degree of poise you display, the personal traits you show and the manner in which you respond.

EXAMINATION SECTION

TEST 1

DIRECTIONS:
Each question or incomplete statement is followed by several suggested answers or completions. Select the one that *BEST* answers the question or completes the statement. *PRINT THE LETTER OF THE CORRECT ANSWER IN THE SPACE AT THE RIGHT.*

Questions 1-5.
DIRECTIONS: Questions 1 through 5 consist of sentences each of which contains one underlined word whose meaning you are to identify by marking your answer either A, B, C, or D.

EXAMPLE
Public employees should avoid <u>unethical</u> conduct.
The word *unethical,* as used in the sentence, means, most nearly,
   A. fine   B. dishonest C. polite   D. sleepy
The correct answer is dishonest (B). Therefore, you should mark your answer B.

1. Employees who can produce a <u>considerable</u> amount of good   1. ...
   work are very valuable.
   The word *considerable,* as used in the sentence, means,
   most nearly,
      A. large   B. potential C. necessary D. frequent
2. No person should <u>assume</u> that he knows more than anyone   2. ...
   else.
   The word *assume,* as used in the sentence, means, most nearly,
      A. verify   B. hope   C. suppose   D. argue
3. The parties decided to <u>negotiate</u> through the night.   3. ...
   The word *negotiate,* as used in the sentence, means, most
   nearly,
      A. suffer   B. play   C. think   D. bargain
4. Employees who have <u>severe</u> emotional problems may create   4. ...
   problems at work.
   The word *severe,* as used in the sentence, means, most nearly,
      A. serious   B. surprising C. several D. common
5. Supervisors should try to be as <u>objective</u> as possible   5. ...
   when dealing with subordinates.
   The word *objective,* as used in the sentence, means, most
   nearly,
      A. pleasant   B. courteous C. fair   D. strict

Questions 6-10.
DIRECTIONS: In each of Questions 6 through 10, *one* word is wrongly used because it is *NOT* in keeping with the intended meaning of the statement. First, decide which word is wrongly used; then select as your answer the right word which really belongs in its place.

EXAMPLE
The employee told ill and requested permission to leave early.
   A. felt   B. considered C. cried   D. spoke
The word "told" is clearly wrong and not in keeping with the intended meaning of the quotation.
The word "felt" (A), however, would clearly convey the intended meaning of the sentence. Option A is correct. Your answer space, therefore, would be marked A.

6. Only unwise supervisors would deliberately overload their   6. ...
   subordinates in order to create themselves look good.
       A. delegate   B. make   C. reduce   D. produce

7. In a democratic organization each employee is seen as a   7. ...
   special individual kind of fair treatment.
       A. granted   B. denial   C. perhaps   D. deserving

8. In order to function the work flow in an office you should 8. ...
   begin by identifying each important procedure being performed in that office.
       A. uniformity B. study   C. standards D. reward

9. A wise supervisor tries to save employees' time by   9. ...
   simplifying forms or adding forms where possible.
       A. taxing B. supervising C. eliminating D. protecting

10. A public agency, whenever it changes its program, should 10. ...
    give requirements to the need for retraining its employees.
        A. legislation B. consideration C. permission D. advice

Questions 11-15.

DIRECTIONS: Answer each of Questions 11 through 15 *ONLY* on the basis of the reading passage preceding each question.

11. Things may not always be what they seem to be. Thus,   11. ...
    the wise supervisor should analyze his problems and
    determine whether there is something there that does not
    meet the eye. For example, what may seem on the surface
    to be a personality clash between two subordinates may
    really be a problem of faulty organization, bad communi-
    cation, or bad scheduling.
    Which one of the following statements *BEST* supports this
    passage?
        A. The wise supervisor should avoid personality clashes.
        B. The smart supervisor should figure out what really is
           going on.
        C. Bad scheduling is the result of faulty organization.
        D. The best supervisor is the one who communicates ef-
           fectively.

12. Some supervisors, under the pressure of meeting dead-   12. ...
    lines, become harsh and dictatorial to their subordinates.
    However, the supervisor most likely to be effective in
    meeting deadlines is one who absorbs or cushions pressures
    from above.
    According to the passage, if a supervisor wishes to meet
    deadlines, it is *MOST* important that he
        A. be informative to his superiors
        B. encourage personal initiative among his subordinates
        C. become harsh and dictatorial to his subordinates
        D. protects his subordinates from pressures from above

13. When giving instructions, a supervisor must always make   13. ...
    clear his meaning, leaving no room for misunderstanding.
    For example, a supervisor who tells a subordinate to do a
    task "as soon as possible" might legitimately be under-
    stood to mean either "it's top priority" or "do it when
    you can."
    Which of the following statements is *BEST* supported by the
    passage?
        A. Subordinates will attempt to avoid work by deliberate-
          ly distorting instructions.

    B. Instructions should be short, since brief instructions are the clearest.

    C. Less educated subordinates are more likely to honestly misunderstand instructions.

    D. A supervisor should give precise instructions that cannot be misinterpreted.

14. Practical formulas are often suggested to simplify what   14. ...
a supervisor should know and how he should behave, such
as the four F's (be firm, fair, friendly, and factual).
But such simple formulas are really broad principles, not
necessarily specific guides in a real situation.
According to the passage, simple formulas for supervisory
behavior

    A. are superior to complicated theories and principles

    B. not always of practical use in actual situations

    C. useful only if they are fair and factual

    D. would be better understood if written in clear
language

15. Many management decisions are made far removed from the   15. ...
actual place of operations. Therefore, there is a great
need for reliable reports and records and, the larger the
organization, the greater is the need for such reports and
records.
According to the passage, management decisions made far
from the place of operations are

    A. dependent to a great extent on reliable reports and
records

    B. sometimes in error because of the great distances
involved

    C. generally unreliable because of poor communications

    D. generally more accurate than on-the-scene decisions

16. Assume that you have just been advanced to a supervisory   16. ...
administrative position and have been assigned as supervisor to a new office with subordinates you do not know.
The *BEST* way for you to establish good relations with these
new subordinates would be to

    A. announce that all actions of the previous supervisor
are now cancelled

    B. hold a meeting and warn them that you will not tolerate
loafing on the job

    C. reassign all your subordinates to new tasks on the
theory that a thorough shake-up is good for morale

    D. act fairly and show helpful interest in their work

17. One of your subordinates asks you to let her arrive at   17. ...
work 15 minutes later than usual but leave for the day
15 minutes later than she usually does. This is temporarily
necessary, your subordinate states, because of early morning
medication she must give her sick child.
Which of the following would be the *MOST* appropriate action
for you to take?

    A. *Suggest* to your subordinate that she choose another
family doctor

    B. *Warn* your subordinate that untruthful excuses are not
acceptable

C. *Tell* your subordinate that you will consider the request and let her know very shortly

D. *Deny* the request since late arrival at work interferes with work performance

18. A young newly-hired employee asked his supervisor several 18. ...
times for advice on private financial matters. The supervisor commented, in a friendly manner, that he considered
it undesirable to give such advice.
The supervisor's response was
A. *unwise*; the supervisor missed an opportunity to advise the employee on an important matter
B. *wise*; if the financial advice was wrong, it could
damage the supervisor's relationship with the subordinate
C. *unwise*; the subordinate will take up the matter with
his fellow workers and probably get poor advice
D. *wise*; the supervisor should never advise subordinates
on any matter

19. *Which* of the following is the *MOST* justified reason for   19. ...
a supervisor to pay any serious attention to a subordinate's
off-the-job behavior? The
A. subordinate's life style is different from the supervisor's way of life
B. subordinate has become well-known as a serious painter
of fine art
C. subordinate's work has become very poor as a result of
his or her personal problems
D. subordinate is a reserved person who, at work, seldom
speaks of personal matters

20. One of your subordinates complains to you that you assign 20. ...
him to the least pleasant jobs more often than anyone else.
You are disturbed by this complaint since you believe
you have always rotated such assignments on a fair basis.
Of the following, it would be *BEST* for you to tell the
complaining subordinate that
A. you will review your past assignment records and
discuss the matter with him further
B. complaints to supervisors are not the wise way to
get ahead on the job
C. disciplinary action will follow if the complaint is
not justified
D. he may be correct, but you do not have sufficient
time to verify the complaint

21. Assume that you have called one of your subordinates into 21. ...
your office to talk about the increasing number of careless errors in her work. Until recently, this subordinate
had been doing good work, but this is no longer so. Your
subordinate does not seem to respond to your questions about
the reason for her poor work.
In these circumstances, your *next* step should be to tell her
A. that her continued silence will result in severe
disciplinary action
B. to request an immediate transfer from your unit
C. to return when she is ready to respond
D. to be more open with you so that her work problem
can be identified

22. Assume that you are given a complicated assignment with   22. ...
    a tight deadline set by your superior. Shortly after you
    begin work you realize that, if you are to do a top quality
    job, you cannot possibly meet the deadline.
    In these circumstances, what should be your *FIRST* course of
    action?
    A. *Continue* working as rapidly as possible, hoping that
       you will meet the deadline after all
    B. *Request* the assignment be given to an employee whom
       you believe works faster
    C. *Advise* your superior of the problem and see whether
       the deadline can be extended
    D. *Advise* your superior that the **deadline cannot** be met
       and, therefore, you will not start the job

23. Assume that a member of the public comes to you to com-   23. ...
    plain about a long-standing practice of your agency.
    The complaint seems to be justified.
    Which one of the following is the *BEST* way for you to
    handle this situation?
    A. *Inform* the complainant that you will have the agency
       practice looked into and that he will be advised of
       any action taken
    B. *Listen* politely, express sympathy, and state that
       you see no fault in the practice
    C. *Express* agreement with the practice on the ground
       that it has been in effect for many years
    D. *Advise* the complainant that things will work out well
       in good time

24. One of your subordinates tells you that he sees no good   24. ...
    reason for having departmental safety rules.
    Which one of the following replies would be *BEST* for you
    to make?
    A. Rules are meant to be obeyed without question.
    B. All types of rules are equally important.
    C. Safety rules are meant to protect people from injury.
    D. If a person is careful enough, he doesn't have to ob-
       serve safety rules.

25. Assume that a supervisor, when he issues instructions to   25. ...
    his subordinates, usually names his superior as the source
    of these instructions.
    This practice is, generally,
    A. *wise,* since if things go wrong, the subordinates will
       know whom to blame
    B. *unwise,* since it may give the subordinates the impres-
       sion that the supervisor doesn't really support the
       instructions
    C. *wise,* since it clearly invites the subordinates to go
       to higher authority if they don't like the instructions
    D. *unwise,* since the subordinates may thereby be given
       too much information

5

KEY (CORRECT ANSWERS)

1.	A	11.	B
2.	C	12.	D
3.	D	13.	D
4.	A	14.	B
5.	C	15.	A
6.	B	16.	D
7.	D	17.	C
8.	B	18.	B
9.	C	19.	C
10.	B	20.	A

21. D
22. C
23. A
24. C
25. B

———

TEST 2

DIRECTIONS:
Each question or incomplete statement is followed by several suggested answers or completions. Select the one that *BEST* answers the question or completes the statement. *PRINT THE LETTER OF THE CORRECT ANSWER IN THE SPACE AT THE RIGHT.*

1. An office aide is assigned as a receptionist in a busy   1. ...
office. The office aide often has stretches of idle time
between visitors.
In this situation, the supervisor should
   A. *give* the receptionist non-urgent clerical jobs which
   can quickly be done at the reception desk
   B. *offer* all office aides an opportunity to volunteer for
   this assignment
   C. *eliminate* the receptionist assignment
   D. *continue* the arrangement unchanged, because receptionist
   duties are so important nothing should interfere with
   them

2. A supervisor can *MOST* correctly assume that an employee   2. ...
is not performing up to his usual standard when the em-
ployee does not handle a task as skillfully as
   A. do other employees who have received less training
   B. do similar employees having comparable work experience
   C. he has handled it in several recent instances
   D. the supervisor himself could handle it

3. Assume that you receive a suggestion that you direct all   3. ...
the typists in a typing pool to complete the identical
quantity of work each day.
For you to adopt this suggestion would be
   A. *advisable;* it will demonstrate the absence of supervisory favoritism
   B. *advisable;* all employees in a given title should be
   treated identically
   C. *inadvisable;* a supervisor should decide on work
   standards without interference from others
   D. *inadvisable;* it ignores variations in specific assignments and individual skills

4. A certain supervisor encouraged her subordinates to tell   4. ...
her if they become aware of possible job problems.
This practice is *good MAINLY* because
   A. early awareness of job problems allows more time for
   seeking solutions
   B. such expected job problems may not develop
   C. the supervisor will be able to solve the job problem
   without consulting other people
   D. the supervisor will be able to place responsibility
   for poor work

5. Some supervisors will discuss with a subordinate how he   5. ...
is doing on the job only when indicating his mistakes or
faults.
Which of the following is the *MOST* likely result of such
a practice?
   A. The subordinate will become discouraged and frustrated.

7

B. Management will set work standards too low.

C. The subordinate will be favorably impressed by the supervisor's frankness.

D. Supervisors will avoid creating any impression of favoritism.

6. A supervisor calls in a subordinate he supervises to discuss the subordinate's annual work performance, indicating his work deficiencies and also praising his job strengths. The subordinate nods his head as if in agreement with his supervisor's comments on both his strengths and weaknesses, but actually says nothing, even after the supervisor has completed his comments.
At this point, the supervisor should

A. end the session and assume that the subordinate agrees completely with the evaluation

B. end the session, since all the subordinate's good and bad points have been identified

C. ask the subordinate whether the criticism is justified, and, if so, what he, the supervisor, can do to help

D. thank the subordinate for being so fair-minded in accepting the criticism in a positive manner

7. The successful supervisor is often one who gives serious attention to his subordinates' needs for job satisfaction.
A supervisor who believes this statement is *MOST* likely to

A. treat all subordinates in an identical manner, irrespective of individual differences

B. permit each subordinate to perform his work as he wishes, within reasonable limits

C. give all subordinates both criticism and praise in equal measure

D. provide each subordinate with as much direct supervision as possible

8. Assume that you are supervising seven subordinates and have been asked by your superior to prepare an especially complex report due today. Its completion will take the rest of the day. You break down the assignment into simple parts and give a different part to each subordinate.
If you were to explain the work of each subordinate to more than one subordinate, your decision would be

A. *wise;* this would prevent boredom

B. *unwise;* valuable time would be lost

C. *wise;* your subordinates would become well-rounded

D. *unwise;* your subordinates would lose their competitive spirit

9. Suppose that an office associate whom you supervise has given you a well-researched report on a problem in an area in which he is expert. However, the report lacks solutions or recommendations. You know this office associate to be fearful of stating his opinions.
In these circumstances, you should tell him that

A. you will seek recommendations on the problem from other, even if less expert, office associates

B. his work is unsatisfactory, in hope of arousing him to greater assertiveness

6. ...

7. ...

8. ...

9. ...

C. you need his advise and expertise to help you reach
   a decision on the problem
D. his uncooperative behavior leaves you no choice but
   to speak to your superior

10. If a supervisor wishes to have the work of his unit com-   10. ...
    pleted on schedule, it is usually *MOST* important to
    A. avoid listening to employees' complaints, thereby
       discouraging dissatisfaction
    B. perform much of the work himself, since he is general-
       ly more capable
    C. observe employees continuously, so they do not slacken
       their efforts
    D. set up the work carefully, then stay informed as to
       how it is moving

11. Of the following agencies, the one *MOST* likely to work   11. ...
    out a proposed budget close to its real needs is
    A. a newly-created agency staffed by inexperienced ad-
       ministrators
    B. funded with a considerable amount of money
    C. an existing agency which intends to install new,
       experimental systems for doing its work
    D. an existing agency which can base its estimate on
       its experience during the past few years

12. Assume that you are asked to prepare a report on the ex-   12. ...
    pected costs and benefits of a proposed new program to be
    installed in your office. However, you are aware that
    certain factors are not really measurable in dollars and
    cents.
    As a result, you should
    A. *identify* the non-measurable factors and state why
       they are important
    B. *assign* a fixed money value to all factors that are
       not really measurable
    C. *recommend* that programs containing non-measurable
       factors should be dropped
    D. *assume* that the non-measurable factors are really
       unimportant

13. Assume that you are asked for your opinion as to the   13. ...
    necessity for hiring more employees to perform certain
    revenue-producing work in your office.
    The information that you will *MOST* likely need in giving
    an informed opinion is
    A. whether public opinion would favor hiring additional
       employees
    B. an estimate of the probable additional revenue com-
       pared with the additional personnel costs
    C. the total cots of all city operations in contrast to
       all city revenues
    D. the method by which present employees would be selected
       for promotion in an expanded operation

14. The *most* reasonable number of subordinates for a super- 14. ...
    visor to have is *BEST* determined by the
    A. average number of subordinates other supervisors have
    B. particular responsibilities given to the supervisor

C. supervisor's educational background
D. personalities of the subordinates assigned to the supervisor

15. Most subordinates would need less supervision if they   15. ...
knew what they were supposed to do.
An *ESSENTIAL first* step in fixing in subordinates' minds exactly what is required of them is to
    A. *require* that supervisors be firm in their supervision of subordinates
    B. *encourage* subordinates to determine their own work standards
    C. *encourage* subordinates to submit suggestions to improve procedures
    D. *standardize* and simplify procedures and logically schedule activities

16. Assume that you have been asked to recommend an appro-   16. ...
priate office layout to correspond with a just completed office reorganization.
Which of the following is it *MOST* advisable to recommend?
    A. *Allocate* most of the space for traffic flow
    B. *Use* the center area only for traffic flow
    C. *Situate* close to each other those units whose work is closely related
    D. *Group* in an out-of-the-way corner the supply and file cabinets

17. Although an organization chart will illustrate the formal 17. ...
structure of an agency, it will seldom show a true picture of its actual workings.
Which of the following *BEST* explains this statement?
Organization charts
    A. are often prepared by employees who may exaggerate their own importance
    B. usually show titles and sometimes names rather than the actual contacts and movements between employees
    C. are likely to discourage the use of official titles, and in so doing promote greater freedom in human relations
    D. usually show the informal arrangements and dealings between employees

18. Assume that a supervisor of a large unit has a variety   18. ...
of tasks to perform, and that he gives each of his subordinates just one set of tasks to do. He never rotates subordinates from one set of tasks to another.
Which one of the following is the *MOST* likely *advantage* to be gained by this practice?
    A. Each subordinate will get to know all the tasks of the unit.
    B. The subordinate will be encouraged to learn all they can about all the unit's tasks.
    C. Each subordinate will become an expert in his particular set of tasks.
    D. The subordinates will improve their opportunities for promotion.

19. Listed below are four steps commonly used in trying to   19. ...
    solve administrative problems. These four steps are not
    listed in the order in which they normally would be taken.
    If they were listed in the proper order, which step should
    be taken *FIRST*?
      I. Choosing the most practical solution to the problem
     II. Analyzing the essential facts about the problem
    III. Correctly identifying the problem
     IV. Following up to see if the solution chosen really works
    The *CORRECT* answer is:
       A. III   B. I   C. II   D. IV
20. Assume that another agency informally tells you that   20. ...
    most of your agency's reports are coming to them with
    careless errors made by many of your office aides.
    Which one of the following is *MOST* likely to solve this
    problem?
       A. *Require* careful review of all outgoing reports by the
          supervisors of the office aides
       B. *Request* the other agency to make necessary corrections
          whenever such errors come to their attention
       C. *Ask* the other agency to submit a written report on
          this situation
       D. *Establish* a small unit to review all reports received
          from other agencies
21. Assume that you supervise an office which gets two kinds 21. ...
    of work. One kind is high-priority and must be done within
    two days. The other kind of work must be done within two
    weeks.
    Which one of the following instructions would be *MOST* rea-
    sonable for you to give to your subordinates in this office?
       A. If a backlog builds up during the day, clean the back-
          log up first, regardless of priority
       B. Spend half the day doing priority work and the other
          half doing non-priority work
       C. Generally do the priority work first as soon as it
          is received
       D. Usually do the work in the order in which it comes
          in, priority or non-priority
22. An experienced supervisor should do advance planning of   22. ...
    his subordinates' work assignments and schedules.
    Which one of the following is the *BEST* reason for such
    advance planning? It
       A. enables the supervisor to do less supervision
       B. will assure the assignment of varied duties
       C. will make certain a high degree of discipline
          among subordinates
       D. helps make certain that essential operations are
          adequately covered
23. Agencies are required to evaluate the performance of   23. ...
    their employees.
    Which one of the following would generally be *POOR*
    evaluation practice by an agency rater? The rater
       A. regularly observes the performance of the employee
          being rated

11

B. in evaluating the employee, acquaints himself
with the employee's job

C. uses objective standards in evaluating the employee
being rated

D. uses different standards in evaluating men and women

24. A good supervisor should have a clear idea of the quanti- 24. ...
ty and quality of his subordinates' work.
Which one of the following sources would normally provide
a supervisor with the *LEAST* reliable information about a
subordinate's work performance?

A. Discussion with a friend of the subordinate

B. Comments by other supervisors who have worked recently
with the subordinate

C. Opinions of fellow workers who work closely with the
subordinate on a daily basis

D. Comparison with work records of others doing similar
work during the same period of time

25. In order to handle the ordinary work of an office, a.   25. ...
supervisor sets up standard work procedures.
The *MOST* likely benefit of this is to reduce the need
to

A. motivate employees to do superior work

B. rethink what has to be done every time a routine
matter comes up

C. keep records and write reports

D. change work procedures as new situations come up

KEY (CORRECT ANSWERS)

1. A		11. D	
2. C		12. A	
3. D		13. B	
4. A		14. B	
5. A		15. D	
6. C		16. C	
7. B		17. B	
8. B		18. C	
9. C		19. A	
10. D		20. A	

21. C
22. D
23. D
24. A
25. B

EXAMINATION SECTION
TEST 1

DIRECTIONS: Each question or incomplete statement is followed by several suggested answers or completions. Select the one that BEST answers the question or completes the statement. *PRINT THE LETTER OF THE CORRECT ANSWER IN THE SPACE AT THE RIGHT.*

1. In almost every organization, there is a nucleus of highly   1.___
   important functions commonly designated as *management*.
   Which of the following statements BEST characterizes
   management?
   A. Getting things done through others
   B. The highest level of intelligence in any organization
   C. The process whereby democratic and participative
      activities are maximized
   D. The *first among equals*

2. Strategies in problem-solving are important to anyone   2.___
   aspiring to advancement in the field of administration.
   Which of the following is BEST classified as the first
   step in the process of problem-solving?
   A. Collection and organization of data
   B. The formulation of a plan
   C. The definition of the problem
   D. The development of a method and methodology

3. One of the objectives of preparing a budget is to   3.___
   A. create optimistic goals which each department can
      attempt to meet
   B. create an overall company goal by combining the budgets
      of the various departments
   C. be able to compare planned expenditures against actual
      expenditures
   D. be able to identify accounting errors

4. The rise in demand for *systems* personnel in industrial and   4.___
   governmental organizations over the past five years has
   been extraordinary.
   In which of the following areas would a *systems* specialist
   assigned to an agency be LEAST likely to be of assistance?
   A. Developing, recommending, and establishing an effec-
      tive cost and inventory system
   B. Development and maintenance of training manuals
   C. Reviewing existing work procedures and recommending
      improvements
   D. Development of aptitude tests for new employees

5. Management experts have come to the conclusion that the   5.___
   traditional forms of motivation used in industry and government, which emphasize authority over and economic rewards
   for the employee, are no longer appropriate.

To which of the following factors do such experts attribute the GREATEST importance in producing this change?
   A. The desire of employees to satisfy material needs has become greater and more complex.
   B. The desire for social satisfaction has become the most important aspect of the job for the average worker.
   C. With greater standardization of work processes, there has been an increase in the willingness of workers to accept discipline.
   D. In general, employee organizations have made it more difficult for management to fire an employee.

6. In preparing a budget, it is usually considered advisable to start the initial phases of preparation at the operational level of management.
   Of the following, the justification that management experts usually advance as MOST reasonable for this practice is that operating managers, as a consequence of their involvement, will
   A. develop a background in finance or accounting
   B. have an understanding of the organizational structure
   C. tend to feel responsible for carrying out budget objectives
   D. have the ability to see the overall financial picture

7. An administrative officer has been asked by his superior to write a concise, factual report with objective conclusions and recommendations based on facts assembled by other researchers.
   Of the following factors, the administrative officer should give LEAST consideration to
   A. the educational level of the person or persons for whom the report is being prepared
   B. the use to be made of the report
   C. the complexity of the problem
   D. his own feelings about the importance of the problem

8. In an agency, upon which of the following is a supervisor's effectiveness MOST likely to depend?
   The
   A. degree to which a supervisor allows subordinates to participate in the decision-making process and the setting of objectives
   B. degree to which a supervisor's style meets management's objectives and subordinates' needs
   C. strength and forcefulness of the supervisor in pursuing his objectives
   D. expertise and knowledge the supervisor has about the specific work to be done

9. For authority to be effective, which of the following is the MOST basic requirement?
   Authority must be
   A. absolute   B. formalized   C. accepted   D. delegated

10. Management no longer abhors the idea of employees taking   10.___
    daily work breaks, but prefers to schedule such breaks
    rather than to allot to each employee a standard amount
    of free time to be taken off during the day as he wishes.
    Which of the following BEST expresses the reason management
    theorists give for the practice of scheduling such breaks?
    A. Many jobs fall into natural work units which are
       scheduled, and the natural time to take a break is
       at the end of the unit.
    B. Taking a scheduled break permits socialization and a
       feeling of accomplishment.
    C. Managers have concluded that scheduling rest periods
       seems to reduce the incidence of unscheduled ones.
    D. Many office workers who really need such breaks are
       hesitant about taking them unless they are scheduled.

11. The computer represents one of the major developments of   11.___
    modern technology. It is widely used in both scientific
    and managerial activities because of its many advantages.
    Which of the following is NOT an advantage gained by
    management in the use of the computer?
    A computer
    A. provides the manager with a greatly enlarged memory
       so that he can easily be provided with data for
       decision making
    B. relieves the manager of basic decision-making respon-
       sibility, thereby giving him more time for directing
       and controlling
    C. performs routine, repetitive calculations with greater
       precision and reliability than employees
    D. provides a capacity for rapid simulations of alterna-
       tive solutions to problem solving

12. A supervisor of a unit in a division is usually respon-   12.___
    sible for all of the following EXCEPT
    A. the conduct of subordinates in the achievement of
       division objectives
    B. maintaining quality standards in the unit
    C. the protection and care of materials and equipment
       in the unit
    D. performing the most detailed tasks in the unit himself

13. You have been assigned to teach a new employee the func-   13.___
    tions and procedures of your office.
    In your introductory talk, which of the following approaches
    is PREFERABLE?
    A. Advise the new employee of the employee benefits and
       services available to him, over and above his salary.
    B. Discuss honestly the negative aspects of departmental
       procedures and indicate methods available to overcome
       them.
    C. Give the new employee an understanding of the general
       purpose of office procedures and functions and of their
       relevance to departmental objectives
    D. Give a basic and detailed explanation of the operations
       of your office, covering all functions and procedures

14. It is your responsibility to assign work to several   14.
    clerks under your supervision. One of the clerks indig-
    nantly refuses to accept an assignment and asks to be
    given something else. He has not yet indicated why he
    does not want the assignment, but is sitting there glaring
    at you, awaiting your reaction.
    Of the following, which is the FIRST action you should take?
       A. Ask the employee into your office in order to reprimand
          him and tell him emphatically that he must accept the
          assignment.
       B. Talk to the employee privately in an effort to find the
          reason for his indignation and refusal, and then base
          your action upon your findings.
       C. Let the matter drop for a day or two to allow the
          employee to cool off before you insist that he accept
          the assignment.
       D. Inform the employee quietly and calmly that as his
          supervisor you have selected him for this assignment
          and that you fully expect him to accept it.

15. Administrative officers are expected to be able to handle   15.__
    duties delegated to them by their supervisors and to be
    able, as they advance in status, to delegate tasks to
    assistants.
    When considering whether to delegate tasks to a subordinate,
    which of the following questions should be LEAST important
    to an administrative officer?
    In the delegated tasks,
       A. how significant are the decisions to be made, and how
          much consultation will be involved?
       B. to what extent is uniformity and close coordination
          of activity required?
       C. to what extent must speedy-on-the-spot decisions be
          made?
       D. to what extent will delegation relieve the administra-
          tive officer of his burden of responsibility?

16. A functional forms file is a collection of forms which   16.__
    are grouped by
       A. purpose   B. department   C. title   D. subject

17. All of the following are reasons to consult a records   17.__
    retention schedule except one.
    Which one is that?
    To determine
       A. whether something should be filed
       B. how long something should stay in file
       C. who should be assigned to filing
       D. when something on file should be destroyed

18. Listed below are four of the steps in the process of pre-   18.__
    paring correspondence for filing.
    If they were to be put in logical sequence, the SECOND
    step would be
       A. preparing cross-reference sheets or cards
       B. coding the correspondence using a classification system

   C. sorting the correspondence in the order to be filed
   D. checking for follow-up action required and preparing
    a follow-up slip

19. New material added to a file folder should USUALLY be   19.___
  inserted
   A. in the order of importance (the most important in front)
   B. in the order of importance (the most important in back)
   C. chronologically (most recent in front)
   D. chronologically (most recent in back)

20. An individual is looking for a name in the white pages of 20.___
  a telephone directory.
  Which of the following BEST describes the system of filing
  found there?
  A(n) ____ file
   A. alphabetic   B. sequential
   C. locator   D. index

21. The MAIN purpose of a tickler file is to   21.___
   A. help prevent overlooking matters that require future
    attention
   B. check on adequacy of past performance
   C. pinpoint responsibility for recurring daily tasks
   D. reduce the volume of material kept in general files

22. Which of the following BEST describes the process of   22.___
  reconciling a bank statement?
   A. Analyzing the nature of the expenditures made by the
    office during the preceding month
   B. Comparing the statement of the bank with the banking
    records maintained in the office
   C. Determining the liquidity position by reading the
    bank statement carefully
   D. Checking the service charges noted on the bank statement

23. From the viewpoint of preserving agency or institutional 23.___
  funds, which of the following is the LEAST acceptable
  method for making a payment?
  A check made out to
   A. cash   B. a company
   C. an individual   D. a partnership

24. In general, the CHIEF economy of using multicopy forms is 24.___
  in
   A. the paper on which the form is printed
   B. printing the form
   C. employee time
   D. carbon paper

25. Suppose your supervisor has asked you to develop a form   25.___
  to record certain information needed.
  The FIRST thing you should do is to
   A. determine the type of data that will be recorded
    repeatedly so that it can be preprinted

B. study the relationship of the form to the job to be accomplished so that the form can be planned
C. determine the information that will be recorded in the same place on each copy of the form so that it can be used as a check
D. find out who will be responsible for supplying the information so that space can be provided for their signatures

26. An administrative officer in charge of a small fund for buying office supplies has just written a check to Charles Laird, a supplier, and has sent the check by messenger to him. A half-hour later, the messenger telephones the administrative officer. He has lost the check.
    Which of the following is the MOST important action for the administrative officer to take under these circumstances?
    A. Ask the messenger to return and write a report describing the loss of the check.
    B. Make a note on the performance record of the messenger who lost the check.
    C. Take the necessary steps to have payment stopped on the check.
    D. Refrain from doing anyting since the check may be found shortly.

26.__

27. A petty cash fund is set up PRIMARILY to
    A. take care of small investments that must be made from time to time
    B. take care of small expenses that arise from time to time
    C. provide a fund to be used as the office wants to use it with little need to maintain records
    D. take care of expenses that develop during emergencies, such as machine breakdowns and fires

27.__

28. Of the following, which is usually the MOST important guideline in writing business letters?
    A letter should be
    A. neat
    B. written in a formalized style
    C. written in clear language intelligible to the reader
    D. written in the past tense

28.__

29. Suppose you are asked to edit a policy statement. You note that personal pronouns like *you*, *we*, and *I* are used freely.
    Which of the following statements BEST applies to this use of personal pronouns?
    It
    A. is proper usage because written business language should not be different from carefully spoken business language
    B. requires correction because it is ungrammatical
    C. is proper because it is clearer and has a warmer tone
    D. requires correction because policies should be expressed in an impersonal manner

29.__

30. Good business letters are coherent.
    To be coherent means to
    A. keep only one unifying idea in the message
    B. present the total message
    C. use simple, direct words for the message
    D. tie together the various ideas in the message

30.___

31. Proper division of a letter into paragraphs requires that
    the writer of business letters should, as much as possible,
    be sure that
    A. each paragraph is short
    B. each paragraph develops discussion of just one topic
    C. each paragraph repeats the theme of the total message
    D. there are at least two paragraphs for every message

31.___

32. An editor is given a letter with this initial paragraph:
    *We have received your letter, which we read with interest,
    and we are happy to respond to your question. In fact,
    we talked with several people in our office to get ideas
    to send to you.*
    Which of the following is it MOST reasonable for the
    editor to conclude?
    The paragraph is
    A. concise
    B. communicating something of value
    C. unnecessary
    D. coherent

32.___

33. As soon as you pick up the phone, a very angry caller
    begins immediately to complain about city agencies and
    red tape. He says that he has been shifted to two or
    three different offices. It turns out that he is seeking
    information which is not immediately available to you.
    You believe you know, however, where it can be found.
    Which of the following actions is the BEST one for you
    to take?
    A. To eliminate all confusion, suggest that the caller
       write the mayor stating explicitly what he wants.
    B. Apologize by telling the caller how busy city agencies
       now are, but also tell him directly that you do not
       have the information he needs.
    C. Ask for the caller's telephone number and assure him
       you will call back after you have checked further.
    D. Give the caller the name and telephone number of the
       person who might be able to help, but explain that
       you are not positive he will get results.

33.___

34. Suppose that one of your duties is to dictate responses
    to routine requests from the public for information. A
    letter writer asks for information which, as expressed in
    a one-sentence, explicit agency rule, cannot be given out
    to the public.
    Of the following ways of answering the letter, which is
    the MOST efficient?
    A. Quote verbatim that section of the agency rules which
       prohibits giving this information to the public.

34.___

    B. Without quoting the rule, explain why you cannot accede to the request and suggest alternative sources.

    C. Describe how carefully the request was considered before classifying it as subject to the rule forbidding the issuance of such information.

    D. Acknowledge receipt of the letter and advise that the requested information is not released to the public.

35. Suppose you assist in supervising a staff which has rather high morale, and your own supervisor asks you to poll the staff to find out who will be able to work overtime this particular evening to help complete emergency work.
Which of the following approaches would be MOST likely to win their cooperation while maintaining their morale?

    A. Tell them that the better assignments will be given only to those who work overtime.

    B. Tell them that occasional overtime is a job requirement.

    C. Assure them they'll be doing you a personal favor.

    D. Let them know clearly why the overtime is needed.

    35._

36. Suppose that you have been asked to write and to prepare for reproduction new departmental vacation leave regulations.
After you have written the new regulations, all of which fit on one page, which one of the following would be the BEST method of reproducing 1000 copies?

    A. An outside private printer, because you can best maintain confidentiality using this technique

    B. Xeroxing, because the copies will have the best possible appearance

    C. Typing carbon copies, because you will be certain that there are the fewest possible errors

    D. The multilith process, because it is quick and neat

    36._

37. Administration is the center, but not necessarily the source, of all ideas for procedural improvement.
The MOST significant implication that this principle bears for the administrative officer is that

    A. before procedural improvements are introduced, they should be approved by a majority of the staff

    B. it is the unique function of the administrative officer to derive and introduce procedural improvements

    C. the administrative officer should derive ideas and suggestions for procedural improvement from all possible sources, introducing any that promise to be effective

    D. the administrative officer should view employee grievances as the chief source of procedural improvements

    37._

38. Your bureau is assigned an important task.   38.___
    Of the following, the function that you, as an administra-
    tive officer, can LEAST reasonably be expected to perform
    under these circumstances is
    A. division of the large job into individual tasks
    B. establishment of *production lines* within the bureau
    C. performance personally of a substantial share of all
       the work
    D. check-up to see that the work has been well done

39. Suppose that you have broken a complex job into its   39.___
    smaller components before making assignments to the
    employees under your jurisdiction.
    Of the following, the LEAST advisable procedure to follow
    from that point is to
    A. give each employee a picture of the importance of his
       work for the success of the total job
    B. establish a definite line of work flow and responsi-
       bility
    C. post a written memorandum of the best method for
       performing each job
    D. teach a number of alternative methods for doing each
       job

40. As an administrative officer, you are requested to draw   40.___
    up an organization chart of the whole department.
    Of the following, the MOST important characteristic of
    such a chart is that it will
    A. include all peculiarities and details of the organiza-
       tion which distinguish it from any other
    B. be a schematic representation of purely administra-
       tive functions within the department
    C. present a modification of the actual departmental
       organization in the light of principles of scientific
       management
    D. present an accurate picture of the lines of authority
       and responsibility

KEY (CORRECT ANSWERS)

1. A	11. B	21. A	31. B
2. C	12. D	22. B	32. C
3. C	13. C	23. A	33. C
4. D	14. B	24. C	34. A
5. D	15. D	25. B	35. D
6. C	16. A	26. C	36. B
7. D	17. C	27. B	37. C
8. B	18. A	28. C	38. C
9. C	19. C	29. D	39. D
10. C	20. A	30. D	40. D

TEST 2

Questions 1-10.

DIRECTIONS: In each of Questions 1 through 10, a pair of related words written in capital letters is followed by four other pairs of words. For each question, select the pair of words which MOST closely expresses a relationship similar to that of the pair in capital letters.

SAMPLE QUESTION:

BOAT - DOCK
    A. airplane - hangar   B. rain - snow
    C. cloth - cotton   D. hunger - food

Choice A is the answer to this sample question since, of the choices given, the relationship between airplane and hangar is most similar to the relationship between boat and dock.

1. AUTOMOBILE - FACTORY   1.___
    A. tea - lemon   B. wheel - engine
    C. pot - flower   D. paper - mill

2. GIRDER - BRIDGE   2.___
    A. petal - flower   B. street- sidewalk
    C. meat - vegetable   D. sun - storm

3. RADIUS - CIRCLE   3.___
    A. brick - building   B. tie - tracks
    C. spoke - wheel   D. axle - tire

4. DISEASE - RESEARCH   4.___
    A. death - poverty   B. speech - audience
    C. problem - conference D. invalid - justice

5. CONCLUSION - INTRODUCTION   5.___
    A. commencement - beginning B. housing - motor
    C. caboose - engine   D. train - cabin

6. SOCIETY - LAW   6
    A. baseball - rules   B. jury - law
    C. cell - prisoner   D. sentence - jury

7. PLAN - ACCOMPLISHMENT   7.___
   A. deed - fact   B. method - success
   C. graph - chart   D. rules - manual

8. ORDER - GOVERNMENT   8.___
   A. chaos - administration   B. confusion - pandemonium
   C. rule - stability   D. despair - hope

9. TYRANNY - FREEDOM   9.___
   A. despot - mob   B. wealth - poverty
   C. nobility - commoners   D. dictatorship - democracy

10. TELEGRAM - LETTER   10.___
    A. hare - tortoise   B. lie - truth
    C. number - word   D. report - research

Questions 11-16.

DIRECTIONS: Answer Questions 11 through 16 SOLELY on the basis of
              the information given in the passage below.

*Inherent in all organized endeavors is the need to resolve the
individual differences involved in conflict. Conflict may be either
a positive or negative factor, since it may lead to creativity,
innovation, and progress, on the one hand, or it may result, on the
other hand, in a deterioration or even destruction of the organization.
Thus, some forms of conflict are desirable, whereas others are
undesirable and ethically wrong.*

*There are three management strategies which deal with inter-
personal conflict. In the "divide-and-rule strategy", management
attempts to maintain control by limiting the conflict to those
directly involved and preventing their disagreement from spreading
to the larger group. The "suppression-of-differences strategy"
entails ignoring conflicts or pretending they are irrelevant. In
the "working-through-differences strategy", management actively
attempts to solve or resolve intergroup or interpersonal conflicts.
Of the three strategies, only the last directly attacks and has the
potential for eliminating the causes of conflict. An essential part
of this strategy, however, is its employment by a committed and
relatively mature management team.*

11. According to the above passage, the *divide-and-rule*   11.___
    strategy for dealing with conflict is the attempt to
    A. involve other people in the conflict
    B. restrict the conflict to those participating in it
    C. divide the conflict into positive and negative factors
    D. divide the conflict into a number of smaller ones

12. The word *conflict* is used in relation to both positive and   12.___
    negative factors in this passage.
    Which one of the following words is MOST likely to describe
    the activity which the word *conflict*, in the sense of the
    passage, implies?
       A. Competition   B. Cooperation
       C. Confusion   D. Aggression

13. According to the above passage, which one of the following 13.
    characteristics is shared by both the *suppression-of-
    differences strategy* and the *divide-and-rule strategy*?
    A. Pretending that conflicts are irrelevant
    B. Preventing conflicts from spreading to the group
       situation
    C. Failure to directly attack the causes of conflict
    D. Actively attempting to resolve interpersonal conflict

14. According to the above passage, the successful resolution 14. ___
    of interpersonal conflict requires
    A. allowing the group to mediate conflicts between two
       individuals
    B. division of the conflict into positive and negative
       factors
    C. involvement of a committed, mature management team
    D. ignoring minor conflicts until they threaten the
       organization

15. Which can be MOST reasonably inferred from the above 15. ___
    passage?
    A conflict between two individuals is LEAST likely to
    continue when management uses
    A. the *working-through-differences strategy*
    B. the *suppression-of-differences strategy*
    C. the *divide-and-rule strategy*
    D. a combination of all three strategies

16. According to the above passage, a desirable result of 16. ___
    conflict in an organization is when conflict
    A. exposes production problems in the organization
    B. can be easily ignored by management
    C. results in advancement of more efficient managers
    D. leads to development of new methods

Questions 17-23.

DIRECTIONS: Answer Questions 17 through 23 SOLELY on the basis of
              the information given in the passage below.

*Modern management places great emphasis on the concept of
communication. The communication process consists of the steps
through which an idea or concept passes from its inception by one
person, the sender, until it is acted upon by another person, the
receiver. Through an understanding of these steps and some of the
possible barriers that may occur, more effective communication may
be achieved. The first step in the communication process is ideation
by the sender. This is the formation of the intended content of the
message he wants to transmit. In the next step, encoding, the sender
organizes his ideas into a series of symbols designed to communicate
his message to his intended receiver. He selects suitable words or
phrases that can be understood by the receiver, and he also selects
the appropriate media to be used -- for example, memorandum, conference, etc. The third step is transmission of the encoded message
through selected channels in the organizational structure. In the
fourth step, the receiver enters the process by tuning in to receive*

the message. If the receiver does not function, however, the message is lost. For example, if the message is oral, the receiver must be a good listener. The fifth step is decoding of the message by the receiver, as for example, by changing words into ideas. At this step, the decoded message may not be the same idea that the sender originally encoded because the sender and receiver have different perceptions regarding the meaning of certain words. Finally, the receiver acts or responds. He may file the information, ask for more information, or take other action. There can be no assurance, however, that communication has taken place unless there is some type of feedback to the sender in the form of an acknowledgement that the message was received.

17. According to the above passage, *ideation* is the process   17.____
    by which the
    A. sender develops the intended content of the message
    B. sender organizes his ideas into a series of symbols
    C. receiver tunes in to receive the message
    D. receiver decodes the message

18. In the last sentence of the passage, the word *feedback*   18.____
    refers to the process by which the sender is assured that
    the
    A. receiver filed the information
    B. receiver's perception is the same as his own
    C. message was received
    D. message was properly interpreted

19. Which one of the following BEST shows the order of the   19.____
    steps in the communication process as described in the
    passage?
       A. 1 - ideation   2 - encoding
          3 - decoding   4 - transmission
          5 - receiving   6 - action
          7 - feedback to the sender

       B. 1 - ideation   2 - encoding
          3 - transmission   4 - decoding
          5 - receiving   6 - action
          7 - feedback to the sender

       C. 1 - ideation   2 - decoding
          3 - transmission   4 - receiving
          5 - encoding   6 - action
          7 - feedback to the sender

       D. 1 - ideation   2 - encoding
          3 - transmission   4 - receiving
          5 - decoding   6 - action
          7 - feedback to the sender

20. Which one of the following BEST expresses the main theme   20.____
    of the passage?
       A. Different individuals have the same perceptions
          regarding the meaning of words.

B. An understanding of the steps in the communication process may achieve better communication.
C. Receivers play a passive role in the communication process.
D. Senders should not communicate with receivers who transmit feedback.

21. The above passage implies that a receiver does NOT func-   21.__
    tion properly when he
    A. transmits feedback   B. files the information
    C. is a poor listener   D. asks for more information

22. Which of the following, according to the above passage,   22.__
    is included in the SECOND step of the communication process?
    A. Selecting the appropriate media to be used in trans-
       mission
    B. Formulation of the intended content of the message
    C. Using appropriate media to respond to the receiver's
       feedback
    D. Transmitting the message through selected channels
       in the organization

23. The above passage implies that the *decoding process* is   23.__
    MOST NEARLY the reverse of the ____ process.
    A. transmission   B. receiving
    C. feedback   D. encoding

Questions 24-27.

DIRECTIONS: Answer Questions 24 through 27 SOLELY on the basis of
              the information given in the paragraph below.

A personnel researcher has at his disposal various approaches for obtaining information, analyzing it, and arriving at conclusions that have value in predicting and affecting the behavior of people at work. The type of method to be used depends on such factors as the nature of the research problem, the available data, and the attitudes of those people being studied to the various kinds of approaches. While the experimental approach, with its use of control groups, is the most refined type of study, there are others that are often found useful in personnel research. Surveys, in which the researcher obtains facts on a problem from a variety of sources, are employed in research on wages, fringe benefits, and labor relations. Historical studies are used to trace the development of problems in order to understand them better and to isolate possible causative factors. Case studies are generally developed to explore all the details of a particular problem that is representative of other similar problems. A researcher chooses the most appropriate form of study for the problem he is investigating. He should recognize, however, that the experimental method, commonly referred to as the scientific method, if used validly and reliably, gives the most conclusive results.

24. The above statement discusses several approaches used to   24.____
    obtain information on particular problems.
    Which of the following may be MOST reasonably concluded
    from the paragraph?
    A(n)
       A. historical study cannot determine causative factors
       B. survey is often used in research on fringe benefits
       C. case study is usually used to explore a problem that
          is unique and unrelated to other problems
       D. experimental study is used when the scientific
          approach to a problem fails

25. According to the above paragraph, all of the following   25.____
    are factors that may determine the type of approach a
    researcher uses EXCEPT
       A. the attitudes of people toward being used in control
          groups
       B. the number of available sources
       C. his desire to isolate possible causative factors
       D. the degree of accuracy he requires

26. The words *scientific method*, used in the last sentence   26.____
    of the paragraph, refer to a type of study which, according
    to the paragraph,
       A. uses a variety of sources
       B. traces the development of problems
       C. uses control groups
       D. analyzes the details of a representative problem

27. Which of the following can be MOST reasonably concluded   27.____
    from the above paragraph?
    In obtaining and analyzing information on a particular
    problem, a researcher employs the method which is the
       A. most accurate   B. most suitable
       C. least expensive   D. least time-consuming

Questions 28-31.

DIRECTIONS: The graph below indicates at 5-year intervals the
number of citations issued for various offenses from
the year 1950 to the year 1970. Answer Questions 28
through 31 according to the information given in this
graph.

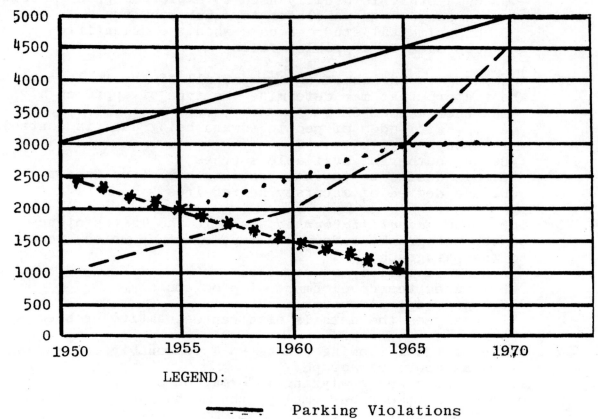

LEGEND:

———————   Parking Violations

— — —   Drug Use

· · · ·   Dangerous Weapons

✱✱✱✱   Improper Dress

28.   Over the 20-year period, which offense shows an AVERAGE   28.___
rate of increase of more than 150 citations per year?
    A. Parking Violations   B. Dangerous Weapons
    C. Drug Use   D. None of the above

29.   Over the 20-year period, which offense shows a CONSTANT   29.___
rate of increase or decrease?
    A. Parking Violations   B. Drug Use
    C. Dangerous Weapons   D. Improper Dress

30.   Which offense shows a TOTAL INCREASE OR DECREASE of 50%   30.
for the full 20-year period?
    A. Parking Violations   B. Drug Use
    C. Dangerous Weapons   D. Improper Dress

31. The percentage increase in total citations issued from   31.___
    1955 to 1960 is MOST NEARLY
       A. 7%   B. 11%   C. 21%   D. 41%

Questions 32-35.

DIRECTIONS: The chart below shows the annual average number of
               administrative actions completed for the four divisions
               of a bureau. Assume that the figures remain stable
               from year to year.

               Answer Questions 32 through 35 SOLELY on the basis of
               information given in the chart.

Administrative Actions	DIVISIONS				Totals
	W	X	Y	Z	
Telephone Inquiries Answered	8,000	6,800	7,500	4,800	27,100
Interviews Conducted	500	630	550	500	2,180
Applications Processed	15,000	18,000	14,500	9,500	57,000
Letters Typed	2,500	4,400	4,350	3,250	14,500
Reports Completed	200	250	100	50	600
Totals	26,200	30,080	27,000	18,100	101,380

32. In which division is the number of Applications Processed   32.___
    the GREATEST percentage of the total Administrative
    Actions for that division?
       A. W   B. X   C. Y   D. Z

33. The bureau chief is considering a plan that would consoli-   33.___
    date the typing of letters in a separate unit. This unit
    would be responsible for the typing of letters for all
    divisions in which the number of letters typed exceeds
    15% of the total number of Administrative Actions.
    Under this plan, which of the following divisions would
    CONTINUE to type its own letters?
       A. W and X   B. W, X, and Y
       C. X and Y   D. X and Z

34. The setting up of a central information service that
    would be capable of answering 25% of the whole bureau's
    telephone inquiries is under consideration. Under such
    a plan, the divisions would gain for other activities that
    time previously spent on telephone inquiries.
    Approximately how much total time would such a service
    gain for all four divisions if it requires 5 minutes to
    answer the average telephone inquiry? _____ hours.
       A. 500   B. 515   C. 565   D. 585

34.

35. Assume that the rate of production shown in the table can
    be projected as accurate for the coming year and that
    monthly output is constant for each type of administrative
    action within a division. Division Y is scheduled to work
    exclusively on a 4-month long special project during that
    year. During the period of the project, Division Y's
    regular workload will be divided evenly among the remaining
    divisions.
    Using the figures in the table, what would be MOST NEARLY
    the percentage increase in the total Administrative Actions
    completed by Division Z for the year?
       A. 8%   B. 16%   C. 25%   D. 50%

35.___

36. You have conducted a traffic survey at 10 two-lane
    bridges and find the traffic between 4:30 and 5:30 P.M.
    averages 665 cars per bridge that hour. You can't find
    the tabulation sheet for Bridge #7, but you know that
    6066 cars were counted at the other 9 bridges.
    Determine from this how many must have been counted at
    Bridge #7.
       A. 584   B. 674   C. 665   D. 607

36.___

37. You pay temporary help $5.60 per hour and regular
    employees $6.00 per hour. Your workload is temporarily
    heavy, so you need 20 hours of extra regular employees'
    time to catch up. If you do this on overtime, you must
    pay time-and-a-half. If you use temporary help, it takes
    25% more time to do the job.
    What is the difference in cost between the two alternatives?
       A. $10 more for temporary   B. $20 more for temporary
       C. $40 more for regular   D. $68 more for regular

37.___

38. An experienced clerk can process the mailing of annual
    forms in 9 days. A new clerk takes 14 days to process
    them.
    If they work together, how many days MOST NEARLY will it
    take to do the processing?
       A. $4\frac{1}{2}$ B. $5\frac{1}{2}$ C. $6\frac{1}{2}$ D. 7

38.___

39. A certain administrative aide is usually able to success-
    fully handle 27% of all telephone inquiries without
    assistance. In a particular month, he receives 1200
    inquiries and handles 340 of them successfully on his own.
    How many more inquiries has he handled successfully in
    that month than would have been expected of him based on
    his usual rate?
       A. 10   B. 16   C. 24   D. 44

39.___

40. Suppose that on a scaled drawing of an office building floor, ½ inch represents three feet of actual floor dimensions.
A floor which is, in fact, 75 feet wide and 132 feet long has which of the following dimensions on this scaled drawing? _____ inches wide and _____ inches long.
   A. 9.5; 20.5   B. 12.5; 22
   C. 17; 32   D. 25; 44

40. _____

41. In a division of clerks and stenographers, 15 people are currently employed, 20% of whom are stenographers.
If management plans are to maintain the current number of stenographers, but to increase the clerical staff to the point where 12% of the total staff are stenographers, what is the MAXIMUM number of additional clerks that should be hired to meet these plans?
   A. 3   B. 8   C. 10   D. 12

41. _____

42. Suppose that a certain agency had a 1985 budget of $1,100,500. The 1986 budget was 7% higher than that of 1985, and the 1987 budget was 8% higher than that of 1986. Of the following, which one is MOST NEARLY that agency's budget for 1987?
   A. $1,117,624   B. $1,261,737
   C. $1,265,575   D. $1,271,738

42. _____

Questions 43-50.

DIRECTIONS: Your office keeps a file card record of the work assignments for all the employees in a certain bureau. On each card is the employee's name, a work assignment code number, and the date of this assignment. In this filing system, the employee's name is filed alphabetically, the work assignment code is filed numerically, and the date of the assignment is filed chronologically (earliest date first).

Each of Questions 43 through 50 represents five cards to be filed, numbered (1) through (5) shown in Column I. Each card is made up of the employee's name, a work assignment code number shown in parentheses, and the date of this assignment. The cards are to be filed according to the following rules:

 First: File in alphabetical order;
Second: When two or more cards have the same employee's name, file according to the work assignment number, beginning with the lowest number.
 Third: When two or more cards have the same employee's name and same assignment number, file according to the assignment date beginning with earliest date.

Column II shows the cards arranged in four different orders. Pick the answer (A, B, C, or D) in Column II which shows the cards arranged correctly according to the above filing rules.

SAMPLE QUESTION:

Column I				Column II
(1) Cluney	(486503)	6/17/72		A. 2, 3, 4, 1, 5
(2) Roster	(246611)	5/10/71		B. 2, 5, 1, 3, 4
(3) Altool	(711433)	10/15/72		C. 3, 2, 1, 4, 5
(4) Cluney	(527610)	12/18/71		D. 3, 5, 1, 4, 2
(5) Cluney	(486500)	4/8/72		

The correct way to file the cards is:
(3) Altool   (711433)   10/15/72
(5) Cluney   (486500)   4/8/72
(1) Cluney   (486503)   6/17/72
(4) Cluney   (527610)   12/18/71
(2) Roster   (246611)   5/10/71

The correct filing order is shown by the numbers in front of each name (3, 5, 1, 4, 2). The answer to the sample question is the letter in Column II in front of the numbers 3, 5, 1, 4, 2. This answer is D.

Column I				Column II	
43.	(1) Prichard	(013469)	4/6/71	A. 5, 4, 3, 2, 1	43.
	(2) Parks	(678941)	2/7/71	B. 1, 2, 5, 3, 4	
	(3) Williams	(551467)	3/6/70	C. 2, 1, 5, 3, 4	
	(4) Wilson	(551466)	8/9/67	D. 1, 5, 4, 3, 2	
	(5) Stanhope	(300014)	8/9/67		
44.	(1) Ridgeway	(623809)	8/11/71	A. 5, 1, 3, 4, 2	44.
	(2) Travers	(305439)	4/5/67	B. 5, 1, 3, 2, 4	
	(3) Tayler	(818134)	7/5/68	C. 1, 5, 3, 2, 4	
	(4) Travers	(305349)	5/6/70	D. 1, 5, 4, 2, 3	
	(5) Ridgeway	(623089)	10/9/71		
45.	(1) Jaffe	(384737)	2/19/71	A. 3, 5, 2, 4, 1	45.
	(2) Inez	(859176)	8/8/72	B. 3, 5, 2, 1, 4	
	(3) Ingrahm	(946460)	8/6/69	C. 2, 3, 5, 1, 4	
	(4) Karp	(256146)	5/5/70	D. 2, 3, 5, 4, 1	
	(5) Ingrahm	(946460)	6/4/70		
46.	(1) Marrano	(369421)	7/24/69	A. 1, 5, 3, 4, 2	46.
	(2) Marks	(652910)	2/23/71	B. 3, 5, 4, 2, 1	
	(3) Netto	(556772)	3/10/72	C. 2, 4, 1, 5, 3	
	(4) Marks	(652901)	2/17/72	D. 4, 2, 1, 5, 3	
	(5) Netto	(556772)	6/17/70		
47.	(1) Abernathy	(712467)	6/23/70	A. 5, 3, 1, 2, 4	47.
	(2) Acevedo	(680262)	6/23/68	B. 5, 4, 2, 3, 1	
	(3) Aaron	(967647)	1/17/69	C. 1, 3, 5, 2, 4	
	(4) Acevedo	(680622)	5/14/67	D. 2, 4, 1, 5, 3	
	(5) Aaron	(967647)	4/1/65		

48. (1) Simon   (645219)   8/19/70   A. 4, 1, 2, 5, 3   48.____
    (2) Simon   (645219)   9/2/68   B. 4, 5, 2, 1, 3
    (3) Simons   (645218)   7/7/70   C. 3, 5, 2, 1, 4
    (4) Simms   (646439) 10/12/71   D. 5, 1, 2, 3, 4
    (5) Simon   (645219) 10/16/67

49. (1) Rappaport   (312230)   6/11/71   A. 4, 3, 1, 2, 5   49.____
    (2) Rascio   (777510)   2/9/70   B. 4, 3, 1, 5, 2
    (3) Rappaport   (312230)   7/3/67   C. 3, 4, 1, 5, 2
    (4) Rapaport   (312330)   9/6/70   D. 5, 2, 4, 3, 1
    (5) Rascio   (777501)   7/7/70

50. (1) Johnson   (843250)   6/8/67   A. 1, 3, 2, 4, 5   50.____
    (2) Johnson   (843205)   4/3/70   B. 1, 3, 2, 5, 4
    (3) Johnson   (843205)   8/6/67   C. 3, 2, 1, 4, 5
    (4) Johnson   (843602)   3/8/71   D. 3, 2, 1, 5, 4
    (5) Johnson   (843602)   8/3/70

————

KEY (CORRECT ANSWERS)

1. D	11. B	21. C	31. B	41. C
2. A	12. A	22. A	32. B	42. D
3. C	13. C	23. D	33. A	43. C
4. C	14. C	24. B	34. C	44. A
5. C	15. A	25. D	35. B	45. C
6. A	16. D	26. C	36. A	46. D
7. B	17. A	27. B	37. C	47. A
8. C	18. C	28. C	38. B	48. B
9. D	19. D	29. A	39. B	49. B
10. A	20. B	30. C	40. B	50. D

————

EXAMINATION SECTION
TEST 1

DIRECTIONS: Each question or incomplete statement is followed by several suggested answers or completions. Select the one that BEST answers the question or completes the statement. *PRINT THE LETTER OF THE CORRECT ANSWER IN THE SPACE AT THE RIGHT.*

1. The one of the following which BEST characterizes an agency in which delegation of authority is practiced on an organization-wide level is that the agency is
    A. autocratic
    B. authoritarian
    C. centralized
    D. decentralized

1.___

2. The concept of the *chain of command* is MOST similar to which one of the following concepts?
    A. Span of control
    B. Matrix or task-force organization
    C. Scalar principle
    D. Functional departmentation

2.___

3. The one of the following techniques which is NOT conducive to the establishment of an effective working relationship between employees and supervisors is
    A. periodic discussion of job performance with employees
    B. listening to employees when they discuss their job difficulties
    C. observation of employees on the job, in both individual and group situations, in order to help them with job performance
    D. treating all employees the same with respect to job performance and individual behavior

3.___

4. Which of the following is a valid, commonly-raised objection to the establishment of work standards for office clerical workers?
    A. Routine clerical work is not subject to accurate measurement.
    B. Clerical work standards can only lower employee morale by creating undue pressure to produce work rapidly.
    C. Work standards are not effective tools for planning, scheduling, and routing clerical work.
    D. Some phases of many clerical jobs, such as telephone answering or information gathering, cannot be readily or accurately measured.

4.___

5. Of the following, the feature which is LEAST characteristic of almost all successful staff relationships with line managers is that the staff employee
    A. is primarily a representative of his supervisor

5.___

B. receives a salary at least equal to the average
salary of his supervisor's direct line subordinates
C. relies largely on persuasion to get his ideas put
into effect
D. is prepared to submerge his own personality and his
own desire for recognition and see others often
receive more recognition than he receives

6. The one of the following systems which has, as its principal objective, the storage of items in files so that
they may be readily found when needed is called
    A. information retrieval   B. simulation
    C. critical path   D. PERT
                                          6.___

7. A detailed description of the steps to be taken in order
to accomplish a job is MOST appropriately called a
    A. policy   B. rule   C. procedure   D. principle
                                          7.___

8. In choosing the best place in the executive hierarchy to
which to assign the task of making a certain type of
decision, which one of the following questions should
normally be LEAST important?
    A. Who knows the facts on which the decision will be
based, or who can obtain them most readily?
    B. Who has the most adequate supply of current forms
on which the decision is normally recorded?
    C. Who has the capacity to make sound decisions?
    D. How significant is the decision?
                                          8.___

9. Of the following, the action which is LEAST likely to be
either expressed or implied every time a manager delegates
work to a subordinate is that the manager
    A. creates a need for a new class of positions
    B. indicates what work the subordinate is to do
    C. grants the subordinate some authority
    D. creates an obligation for the subordinate who accepts
the work to try to complete it
                                          9.___

10. Of the following, the LEAST appropriate use of organizational charts is to
    A. depict standard operating procedures
    B. indicate lines of responsibility
    C. indicate the relative level of key positions
    D. portray organizations graphically
                                        10.___

11. The one of the following considerations which is generally
LEAST important in deciding whether to automate a management operation by using a computer is whether the computer
    A. possesses a suitable array of programmed actions
that might be taken
    B. can draw upon available data for information as to
which alternative is best
    C. is already familiar to the staff of the organization
    D. can issue findings in a way that will facilitate the
decision-making process
                                        11.___

12. In evaluating a proposal to establish a library in your   12.___
agency, it is generally considered LEAST necessary to
determine
   A. the average time staff members spend on preparatory
      research when assigned to projects
   B. how often junior professional and technical staff
      members are sent out to *look something up* in a
      local library
   C. how much time and money agency executives devote to
      telephoning around the country seeking information
      before making decisions
   D. the quality of the research done by executives and
      scientists in the agency

13. In determining the number and type of tasks that should   13.___
be combined into a single job, the one of the following
which is normally the LEAST useful factor to consider is
the
   A. benefit of functional specialization
   B. benefit of tall pyramid organization structures in
      increasing decentralization
   C. need for coordination of tasks with each other
   D. effect of the tasks assigned on the morale of the
      employee

14. Of the following, the one which is LEAST likely to be an   14.___
objective of systems and procedures analysis is to
   A. eliminate as many unessential forms and records as
      feasible
   B. simplify forms in content and method of preparation
   C. mechanize repetitive, routine tasks
   D. expand as many of the forms as possible

15. A specific managerial function encompasses all of the   15.___
following: the establishment of an intentional structure
of roles through determination and enumeration of the
activities required to achieve the goals of an enterprise
and each part of it, the grouping of these activities, the
assignment of such groups of activities to a manager, the
delegation of authority to carry them out, and provision
for coordination of authority and informational relationships horizontally and vertically in the organization
structure.
Of the following, the MOST appropriate term for this
entire managerial function is
   A. organizing   B. directing
   C. controlling   D. staffing

16. The optimum number of subordinates that a supervisor can   16.___
supervise effectively generally tends to vary INVERSELY
with the
   A. percentage of the supervisor's time devoted to super-
      vision rather than operations
   B. repetition of activities
   C. degree of centralization of decision-making within the
      supervisor's unit
   D. ability of subordinates

17. Under certain circumstances, a top manager may desire to   17.___
strengthen the position of his staff people by granting
them concurring authority, so that no action may be taken
in a functional area by subordinate line officials until
a designated staff employee agrees to the action. For
example, office managers may have to get the approval of
the agency personnel officer before hiring a new employee.
This approach is likely to be MOST valid under which one
of the following conditions?
   A. The top manager refrains from indicating the grounds
      on which the staff employee may grant or withhold his
      approval of line proposals.
   B. The point of view represented by the staff employee
      is particularly important, and the possible delay in
      action will not be serious.
   C. It is more important to fix specific accountability
      for failure to take appropriate action than for
      wrong actions taken.
   D. The top manager gives speed priority over prudence.

18. The inclusion of the *reason why* by a superior in his   18.___
written orders to his subordinates normally is MOST
likely to
   A. encourage belief by the subordinates in the meaning
      and intent of the order
   B. be a waste of valuable time for both superior and
      subordinates
   C. be useful principally where the superior has no power
      to enforce the order
   D. discourage effective two-way communication between
      superior and subordinates

19. The one of the following which is generally the BEST   19.___
justification for an administrator's search for alternative
methods of attaining a given objective of the unit he heads
is that such search
   A. always turns up a better method of attaining objec-
      tives than that currently in use
   B. helps to make certain that the best method has a
      chance to be found and evaluated
   C. helps to insure that his peers realize that the
      existing method of attaining the objective is not
      the best
   D. is a good way to train the unit's staff in the
      organization's operational procedures

20. *Managing-by-objectives* tends to place PRINCIPAL emphasis   20.___
upon which of the following?
   A. Use of primarily qualitative goals at all management
      levels
   B. Use of trait-appraisal systems based upon personality
      factors
   C. Use of primarily qualitative goals at lower management
      levels as contrasted with primarily quantitative goals
      at higher management levels
   D. Goals which are clear and verifiable

21. Which one of the following BEST identifies the two most   21.___
    important considerations which generally should determine
    the degree of management decentralization desirable in a
    given situation?
    The
    A. age of the subordinate executives to whom decisions
       may be delegated and the number of courses in manage-
       ment that they have completed
    B. number of skills and the competence possessed by
       subordinate executives and the distribution of the
       necessary information to the points of decision
    C. ratio of the salary of the superior executives to the
       salary of the subordinate executives and the number
       of titles on the executive staff
    D. number of titles in the executive staff and the dis-
       tribution of information to those various titles

22. Which one of the following is generally LEAST likely to   22.___
    occur at mid-level management as a result of installing
    an electronic data processing system?
    A. The time that managers will be required to spend on
       the controlling function will increase.
    B. The number of contacts that managers will have with
       subordinates will increase.
    C. Additional time will be needed to train people for
       managerial positions.
    D. There will be an increase in the volume of informa-
       tion presented to managers for analysis.

23. The concept that the major source of managerial authority   23.___
    is derived from the subordinate's acceptance of the
    manager's power is MOST closely identified with
    A. Luther Gulick   B. John D. Mooney
    C. Frederick W. Taylor   D. Chester I. Barnard

24. The one of the following which is generally the principal   24.___
    objection to a pure *functional organization*, as compared
    with a pure *line organization*, is that
    A. there is a tendency to overload intermediate and
       supervisory management at each succeeding level of
       organization with wide and varied duties
    B. authority flows in an unbroken line from top manage-
       ment to the worker
    C. workers must often report to two or more supervisors
    D. there is a lack of specialization at the supervisory
       level

25. The appraisal of subordinates and their performance is an   25.___
    integral part of the supervisor's job. There is wide
    agreement that several basic principles must be taken
    into account by supervisors involved in the appraisal
    process in order to perform this function correctly.
    The one of the statements below which LEAST represents
    a basic principle of the appraisal process is:
    Appraisal(s)
    A. should be based more on performance of definite tasks
       than on personality considerations

B. of long-range potential should rely most heavily on subjective judgment of that potential
C. involves the use of value judgments by the supervisor and does, therefore, require reference to pre-established standards
D. should aim at emphasizing subordinates' strengths rather than weaknesses

26. Of the following, the INITIAL step in the decision-making procedure normally is   26. ___
    A. evaluation of alternatives
    B. implementing the chosen course of action
    C. listing potential solutions
    D. diagnosis and problem definition

27. Management textbooks are LEAST likely to define coordination as   27. ___
    A. a concern for harmonious and unified action directed toward a common objective
    B. the essence of management, since the basic purpose of management is the achievement of harmony of individual effort toward the accomplishment of group goals
    C. the orderly arrangement of group effort to provide unity of action in pursuit of common purpose
    D. the transmittal of messages from senders to receivers, involving acts of persuasion of regulation, or simply the rendering of information

28. A number of important assumptions underlie the modern human relations approach to management and administration. The one of the following which is NOT an assumption integral to the human relations school of thought is that   28. ___
    A. employee participation is essential to higher productivity
    B. employees are motivated solely by monetary factors
    C. teamwork is indispensable for organization growth and survival
    D. free-flow communications must be established and maintained for organizational effectiveness

29. Of the following, the MAIN purpose of systematic manpower planning is to   29. ___
    A. analyze the levels of skill needed by each worker
    B. analyze causes of current vacancies, such as resignations, discharges, retirements, transfers, or promotions
    C. save money by eliminating useless jobs
    D. provide for the continuous and proper staffing of the workforce

30. A Planning-Programming-Budget System (PPBS) is PRIMARILY intended to do which of the following?   30. ___
    A. Improve control through a budgeting-by-line-item system
    B. Plan and program budgets by objective rather than by function

C. Raise money for social welfare programs
D. Reduce budgets by planning and programming unspent
   funds

———

KEY (CORRECT ANSWERS)

1. D	11. C	21. B
2. C	12. D	22. A
3. D	13. B	23. D
4. D	14. D	24. C
5. B	15. A	25. B
6. A	16. C	26. D
7. C	17. B	27. D
8. B	18. A	28. B
9. A	19. B	29. D
10. A	20. D	30. B

———

TEST 2

DIRECTIONS: Each question or incomplete statement is followed by several suggested answers or completions. Select the one that BEST answers the question or completes the statement. *PRINT THE LETTER OF THE CORRECT ANSWER IN THE SPACE AT THE RIGHT.*

1. The one of the following which is a BASIC advantage of microform record system (e.g., microfilm, microfiche) over a conventional filing system is that a microform system
   A. provides a compact method of grouping and systematizing records
   B. provides records which are immediately available without special equipment
   C. eliminates the need for specially trained personnel
   D. eliminates entirely the inadvertent loss of records

1.___

2. In the planning of office space for the various bureaus and divisions of an agency, the one of the following arrangements which is generally considered to be MOST desirable in a conventional layout is to
   A. locate offices where employees do close and tedious work, such as accounting, and also offices of high-level executives away from windows so that distractions will be minimal
   B. locate *housekeeping* offices such as data processing and the mailroom very close to the high executive offices to increase convenience for the executives
   C. locate departments so that the work flow proceeds in an uninterrupted manner
   D. centralize the executive suite for maximum availability and public exposure

2.___

3. Generally, the one of the following that is LEAST likely to be an essential step in a records retention plan is
   A. storing inactive records
   B. checking for accuracy of all records to be retained
   C. classification of all records
   D. making an inventory of all agency records

3.___

4. The PRINCIPAL asset of an office layout diagram, as contrasted with the more abstract organization charts and flowcharts, is that an office layout diagram is
   A. more readily adaptable to strictly conceptual studies
   B. pictorial and therefore easier to understand
   C. suitable for showing both manual and machine processing operations, whereas organization charts and flowcharts may only be used for manual processing operations
   D. better suited for summarizing the number of work units produced at each step

4.___

5. One of the assistants whom you supervise displays apparent   5.___
familiarity toward a businessman who deals with your agency.
This assistant spends more time with this person than the
nature of his business would warrant, and you have observed
that they are occasionally seen leaving the office together
for lunch. In several instances, when this businessman
comes into the office and this assistant is not at his desk,
the businessman will not deal with any other staff member
but will, instead, leave the office and return later when
that particular employee is available.
Of the following courses of action, the FIRST one you should
take is to
   A. audit the agency's books and records pertaining to
      this businessman
   B. rebuke the assistant for unprofessional conduct at the
      next staff meeting and warn him of disciplinary action
      if the practice is not discontinued forthwith
   C. advise your agency head of the action by the business-
      man and the assistant that has been described in the
      above paragraph
   D. reassign the assistant to duties that will not bring
      him into contact with any businessman

6. The one of the following factors which generally is the   6.___
BEST justification for keeping higher inventories of
supplies and equipment is an expected
   A. decline in demand
   B. price increase
   C. decline in prices
   D. increase in interest charges and storage costs

7. Statistical sampling is often used in administrative   7.___
operations PRIMARILY because it enables
   A. administrators to determine the characteristics of
      appointed or elected officials
   B. decisions to be made based on mathematical and
      scientific fact
   C. courses of action to be determined by scientifically-
      based computer programs
   D. useful predictions to be made from relatively small
      samples

8. According to United States Department of Labor figures,   8.___
the PRINCIPAL source of disabling injuries to office
workers is
   A. flying objects and falling objects
   B. striking against equipment
   C. falls and slips
   D. handling materials

9. To expedite the processing of applications issued by your   9.___
agency, you ask your assistant to design a form that will
be used by your typists. After several discussions, he
presents you with a draft that requires the typist to use
23 tabular-stop positions.

Such a form would PROBABLY be considered
A. *undesirable*; typists would now have to soft-roll the platen to make the typing fall on the lines
B. *desirable*; the fill-in operation by typists would be speeded up
C. *undesirable*; proper vertical alignment of data would be made difficult by the number of tabular-stop positions required
D. *desirable*; it would force the typists to utilize the tabular-stop device

Question 10.

DIRECTIONS: Following are five general instructions to file clerks which might appear in the proposed filing manual for an agency:

1. Follow instructions generally; if you have a suggestion for improvement in the filing methods, install it after notifying the file supervisor who will duly authorize a change in the manual.
2. You may discuss the contents of files with fellow employees or outsiders, but do NOT give papers from the file to any person whose duties have no relation to the material requested.
3. All special instructions must be given by the file supervisor. Any problems that arise outside the regular routine of filing must be decided by the file supervisor, not by a fellow clerk.
4. You will not be held responsible for your own errors; thus, refrain from asking other workers for instructions. No one is more interested in helping you in your training than your file supervisor.
5. Speed is the first essential in filing; make it your primary consideration -- quick finding of filed material is the real test of your efficiency.

10. Which of the choices listed below BEST identifies those of the above statements that should or should not be followed by agencies in the functioning of their filing sections?
Instruction(s)_____ should be followed; instructions _____ should not be followed.
   A. 1, 2, 3; 4, 5   B. 3; 1, 2, 4, 5
   C. 2, 4; 1, 3, 5   D. 1, 3; 2, 4, 5

10.___

11. Listed below are five steps in the process of staffing:
   I. Authorization for staffing
  II. Manpower planning
 III. Development of applicant sources
  IV. Evaluation of applicants
   V. Employment decisions and offers

The one of the following sequences which is generally the MOST logical arrangement of the above steps is:
   A. I, II, III, IV, V   B. II, I, III, IV, V
   C. III, I, II, IV, V   D. II, III, I, IV, V

11.___

12. Job enrichment is LEAST likely to lead to 12.___
    A. fewer employee grievances
    B. increased employee productivity
    C. people acting as adjuncts of increased automation
    D. increased employee morale

13. Of the following, programmed instruction would usually be 13.___
MOST effective in teaching
    A. principles of decision-making
    B. technical skills and knowledge
    C. good judgment
    D. executive management ability

14. Assume that a group has been working effectively with a 14.___
contributing nonconformist in its midst.
The BEST of the following reasons for the group to retain
the nonconformist *generally* is that
    A. nonconformists stimulate groups to think
    B. he may be their boss some day
    C. nonconformists usually are fun to work with
    D. another nonconformist will usurp his role

15. The *grievance-arbitration* process involves systematic 15.___
union-management deliberation regarding a complaint that
is work- or contract-related.
An outcome that does NOT result from this process is
    A. a communications channel from the rank-and-file workers
       to higher management is developed or improved
    B. the contract is immediately changed to provide justice
       for both parties
    C. both labor and management identify those parts of the
       contract that need to be clarified and modified in
       subsequent negotiations
    D. the language of the agreement is informally translated
       into understandable terms for the parties bound by it

16. In government, job evaluation is the process of deter- 16.___
mining the relative worth of the various jobs in an
organization so that differential wages can be paid. Job
evaluation is based on several basic assumptions.
Of the assumptions listed below, the MOST questionable is
that
    A. the cash payments in government should be substan-
       tially higher than those in local private industry
    B. it is logical to pay the most for jobs that contrib-
       ute most to the organization
    C. people feel more fairly treated if wages are based
       on the relative worth of their jobs
    D. the best way to achieve the goals of the enterprise
       is to maintain a wage structure based on job worth

17. Of the following, the training method that normally 17.___
provides the instructor with the LEAST *feedback* from the
trainees is
    A. the lecture method
    B. the conference method
    C. simulation or gaming techniques
    D. seminar instruction

18. Insufficient and inappropriate delegation of work assign-   18. ___
ments is MOST often the fault of
   A. subordinates who are unwilling to accept responsibility
   for their own mistakes
   B. a paternal attitude on the part of management
   C. the immediate supervisor
   D. subordinates who are too willing to take on extra
   responsibility

19. As contrasted with expense budgets, capital budgets are   19. ___
MORE likely to
   A. be used for construction of physical facilities
   B. be designed for a shorter time period
   C. include personal service expenditures
   D. include fringe benefits

20. During the first quarter of a year, a division's produc-   20. ___
tion rate was 1.26 man-hours per work unit produced. For
the second quarter of that year, all other factors (e.g.,
size of staff, character of work unit, etc.) remained
constant, except that the manner of reporting production
rate was changed to work units per man-hour instead of
man-hours per work unit. During that second quarter, the
unit's production rate was .89 work units per man-hour.
On the basis of the above information, it would be MOST
NEARLY CORRECT to conclude that the division's production
rate during the second quarter was *approximately* ___ than
during the first quarter.
   A. 30% lower   B. 10% lower
   C. 10% higher   D. 30% higher

Questions 21-22.

DIRECTIONS: Answer Questions 21 and 22 on the basis of the
              following information.

*The five bureaus within a department sent the following budget
requests to the department head:*

      Bureau A - $10 million
      Bureau B - $12 million
      Bureau C - $18 million
      Bureau D - $6 million
      Bureau E - $4 million

*After reviewing all of these requests, the department head
decided to reduce these requests so that they would total only $40
million. He considered the following two options to accomplish this:*

   *Option I - Reduce the requests of Bureaus A, B, and D by an
              equal dollar amount. Reduce the dollar amount
              request of Bureau C by 2½ times the dollar amount
              that he reduces the request of Bureau B. Reduce
              the dollar amount request of Bureau E by ½ of the
              dollar amount that he reduces the request of
              Bureau B.*

Option II - First, reduce the dollar amount request of all
five bureaus by 15%. Then, the remaining reduction
required by the entire department would be achieved
by further reducing the resulting budget requests
of Bureaus B and C by an equal dollar amount each.

21. Under Option I, the dollar amount request for Bureau E,   21.___
    after reduction by the department head, would be MOST
    NEARLY ____ millions.
      A. $1 2/3   B. $2 1/3   C. $3 1/6   D. $3 1/2

22. Under Option II, the dollar amount of the request of   22.___
    Bureau B, after both reductions were made by the department
    head, would be MOST NEARLY ____ millions.
      A. $8   B. $9   C. $10   D. $11

23. The summary or findings of a long management report   23.___
    intended for the typical manager should GENERALLY appear
      A. at the very beginning of the report
      B. at the end of the report
      C. throughout the report
      D. in the middle of the report

24. Of the following, the BIGGEST disadvantage in allowing   24.___
    a free flow of communications in an agency is that such
    a free flow
      A. decreases creativity
      B. increases the use of the *grapevine*
      C. lengthens the chain of command
      D. reduces the executive's power to direct the flow of
         information

25. A downward flow of authority in an organization is one   25.___
    example of ____ communications.
      A. horizontal   B. informal
      C. circular   D. vertical

26. Workers who belong to a cohesive group are GENERALLY   26.___
    thought to
      A. have more job-related anxieties than those who do not
      B. be less well-adjusted than those who do not
      C. derive little satisfaction from the group
      D. conform to group norms more closely than those in
         noncohesive groups

27. The one of the following which BEST exemplifies negative   27.___
    motivation is
      A. a feeling on the part of the worker that the work is
         significant
      B. monetary rewards offered the worker for high levels
         of output
      C. reducing or withholding the worker's incentive rewards
         when performance is mediocre
      D. nonmonetary rewards given the worker, such as
         publicizing a good suggestion

28. Of the following, the one that would be MOST likely to block effective communication is
    A. concentration only on the issues at hand
    B. lack of interest or commitment
    C. use of written reports
    D. use of charts and graphs

28. ___

29. Many functions formerly centralized in a department of personnel have been decentralized, in whole or in part, to operating agencies.
    The one of the following personnel functions which has been LEAST decentralized is
    A. position evaluation
    B. investigation of non-competitive employees
    C. investigation of competitive employees
    D. jurisdictional classification

29. ___

30. In making a position analysis for a duties classification, the one of the following factors which MUST be considered is the ____ the incumbent.
    A. capabilities of
    B. qualifications of
    C. efficiency attained by
    D. responsibility assigned to

30. ___

KEY (CORRECT ANSWERS)

1. A	11. B	21. C
2. C	12. C	22. B
3. B	13. B	23. A
4. B	14. A	24. D
5. C	15. B	25. D
6. B	16. A	26. D
7. D	17. A	27. C
8. C	18. C	28. B
9. C	19. A	29. D
10. B	20. C	30. D

EXAMINATION SECTION

DIRECTIONS: Each question or incomplete statement is followed by several suggested answers or completions. Select the one that BEST answers the question or completes the statement. *PRINT THE LETTER OF THE CORRECT ANSWER IN THE SPACE AT THE RIGHT.*

Questions 1-5.

DIRECTIONS: Each of Questions 1 through 5 consists of a passage which contains one word that is incorrectly used because it is not in keeping with the meaning that the quotation is evidently intended to convey. Determine which word is incorrectly used. Select from the choices lettered A, B, C, and D the word which, when substituted for the incorrectly used word, would BEST help to convey the meaning of the quotation.

1. Whatever the method, the necessity to keep up with the dynamics of an organization is the point on which many classification plans go awry. The budgetary approach to "positions," for example, often leads to using for recruitment and pay purposes a position authorized many years earlier for quite a different purpose than currently contemplated – making perhaps the title, the class, and the qualifications required inappropriate to the current need. This happens because executives overlook the stability that takes place in job duties and fail to reread an initial description of the job before saying, as they scan a list of titles, "We should fill this position right away." Once a classification plan is adopted, it is pointless to do anything less than provide for continuous, painstaking maintenance on a current basis, else once different positions that have actually become similar to each other remain in different classes, and some former cognates that have become quite different continue in the same class. Such a program often seems expensive. But to stint too much on this out-of-pocket cost may create still higher hidden costs growing out of lowered morale, poor production, delayed operating programs, excessive pay for simple work, and low pay for responsible work (resulting in poorly qualified executives and professional men) – all normal concomitants of inadequate, hasty, or out-of-date classification.

    A. evolution
    C. disapproved
    B. personnel
    D. forward

1.____

2. At first sight, it may seem that there is little or no difference between the usableness of a manual and the degree of its use. But there is a difference. A manual may have all the qualities which make up the usable manual and still not be used. Take this instance as an example: Suppose you have a satisfactory manual but issue instructions from day to day through the avenue of bulletins, memorandums, and other informational releases. Which will the employee use, the manual or the bulletin which passes over his desk? He will, of course, use the latter, for some obsolete material will not be contained in this manual. Here we have a theoretically usable manual which is unused because of the other avenues by which procedural information may be issued.

    A. countermand
    C. intentional
    B. discard
    D. worthwhile

2.____

3. By reconcentrating control over its operations in a central headquarters, a firm is able to   3.__
extend the influence of automation to many, if not all, of its functions – from inventory and
payroll to production, sales, and personnel. In so doing, businesses freeze all the elements of the corporate function in their relationship to one another and to the overall
objectives of the firm. From this total systems concept, companies learn that computers
can accomplish much more than clerical and accounting jobs. Their capabilities can be
tapped to perform the traditional applications (payroll processing, inventory control,
accounts payable, and accounts receivable) as well as newer applications such as spotting deviations from planned programs (exception reporting), adjusting planning schedules, forecasting business trends, simulating market conditions, and solving production
problems. Since the office manager is a manager of information and each of these applications revolves around the processing of data, he must take an active role in studying
and improving the system under his care.

    A. maintaining   B. inclusion
    C. limited   D. visualize

4. In addition to the formal and acceptance theories of the source of authority, although per-   4.__
haps more closely related to the latter, is the belief that authority is generated by personal qualifies of technical competence. Under this heading is the individual who has
made, in effect, subordinates of others through sheer force of personality, and the engi-
neer or economist who exerts influence by furnishing answers or sound advice. These
may have no actual organizational authority, yet their advice may be so eagerly sought
and so unerringly followed that it appears to carry the weight of an order.
But, above all, one cannot discount the importance of formal authority with its institutional foundations. Buttressed by the qualities of leadership implicit in the acceptance
theory, formal authority is basic to the managerial job. Once abrogated, it may be delegated or withheld, used or misused, and be effective in capable hands or be ineffective
in inept hands.

    A. selected   B. delegation
    C. limited   D. possessed

5. Since managerial operations in organizing, staffing, directing, and controlling are   5.__
designed to support the accomplishment of enterprise objectives, planning logically pre-
cedes the execution of all other managerial functions. Although all the functions inter-
mesh in practice, planning is unique in that it establishes the objectives necessary for all
group effort. Besides, plans must be made to accomplish these objectives before the
manager knows what kind of organization relationships and personal qualifications are
needed, along which course subordinates are to be directed, and what kind of control is
to be applied. And, of course, each of the other managerial functions must be planned if
they are to be effective.
Planning and control are inseparable – the Siamese twins of management. Unplanned
action cannot be controlled, for control involves keeping activities on course by correct-
ing deviations from plans. Any attempt to control without plans would be meaningless,
since there is no way anyone can tell whether he is going where he wants to go – the
task of control – unless first he knows where he wants to go – the task of planning.
Plans thus preclude the standards of control.

    A. coordinating   B. individual
    C. furnish   D. follow

Questions 6-7.

DIRECTIONS: Answer Questions 6 and 7 SOLELY on the basis of information given in the following paragraph.

In-basket tests are often used to assess managerial potential. The exercise consists of a set of papers that would be likely to be found in the in-basket of an administrator or manager at any given time, and requires the individuals participating in the examination to indicate how they would dispose of each item found in the in-basket. In order to handle the in-basket effectively, they must successfully manage their time, refer and assign some work to subordinates, juggle potentially conflicting appointments and meetings, and arrange for follow-up of problems generated by the items in the in-basket. In other words, the in-basket test is attempting to evaluate the participants' abilities to organize their work, set priorities, delegate, control, and make decisions.

6. According to the above paragraph, to succeed in an in-basket test, an administrator must   6.____

   A. be able to read very quickly
   B. have a great deal of technical knowledge
   C. know when to delegate work
   D. arrange a lot of appointments and meetings

7. According to the above paragraph, all of the following abilities are indications of managerial potential EXCEPT the ability to   7.____

   A. organize and control   B. manage time
   C. write effective reports   D. make appropriate decisions

Questions 8-9.

DIRECTIONS: Answer Questions 8 and 9 SOLELY on the basis of information given in the following paragraph.

One of the biggest mistakes of government executives with substantial supervisory responsibility is failing to make careful appraisals of performance during employee probationary periods. Many a later headache could have been avoided by prompt and full appraisal during the early months of an employee's assignment. There is not much more to say about this except to emphasize the common prevalence of this oversight, and to underscore that for its consequences, which are many and sad, the offending managers have no one to blame but themselves.

8. According to the above passage, probationary periods are   8.____

   A. a mistake, and should not be used by supervisors with large responsibilities
   B. not used properly by government executives
   C. used only for those with supervisory responsibility
   D. the consequence of management mistakes

9. The one of the following conclusions that can MOST appropriately be drawn from the
   above passage is that

    A. management's failure to appraise employees during their probationary period is a
   common occurrence
    B. there is not much to say about probationary periods, because they are unimportant
    C. managers should blame employees for failing to use their probationary periods
   properly
    D. probationary periods are a headache to most managers

9.___

Questions 10-12.

DIRECTIONS: Answer Questions 10 through 12 SOLELY on the basis of information given in
                the following paragraph.

*The common sense character of the merit system seems so natural to most Americans
that many people wonder why it should ever have been inoperative. After all, the American
economic system, the most phenomenal the world has ever known, is also founded on a rug-
ged selective process which emphasizes the personal qualities of capacity, industriousness,
and productivity. The criteria may not have always been appropriate and competition has not
always been fair, but competition there was, and the responsibilities and the rewards – with
exceptions, of course – have gone to those who could measure up in terms of intelligence,
knowledge, or perseverance. This has been true not only in the economic area, in the money-
making process, but also in achievement in the professions and other walks of life.*

10. According to the above paragraph, economic rewards in the United States have

    A. always been based on appropriate, fair criteria
    B. only recently been based on a competitive system
    C. not gone to people who compete too ruggedly
    D. usually gone to those people with intelligence, knowledge, and perseverance

10.___

11. According to the above passage, a merit system is

    A. an unfair criterion on which to base rewards
    B. unnatural to anyone who is not American
    C. based only on common sense
    D. based on the same principles as the American economic system

11.___

12. According to the above passage, it is MOST accurate to say that

    A. the United States has always had a civil service merit system
    B. civil service employees are very rugged
    C. the American economic system has always been based on a merit objective
    D. competition is unique to the American way of life

12.___

Questions 13-15.

DIRECTIONS: The management study of employee absence due to sickness is an effective tool in planning. Answer Questions 13 through 15 SOLELY on the data given below.

Number of days absent per worker (sickness)	1	2	3	4	5	6	7	8 or Over
Number of workers	76	23	6	3	1	0	1	0

Total Number of Workers: 400
Period Covered: January 1 - December 31

13. The total number of man days lost due to illness was

    A. 110   B. 137   C. 144   D. 164

13.____

14. What percent of the workers had 4 or more days absence due to sickness?

    A. .25%   B. 2.5%   C. 1.25%   D. 12.5%

14.____

15. Of the 400 workers studied, the number who lost no days due to sickness was

    A. 190   B. 236   C. 290   D. 346

15.____

Questions 16-18.

DIRECTIONS: In the graph below, the lines labeled "A" and "B" represent the cumulative progress in the work of two file clerks, each of whom was given 500 consecutively numbered applications to file in the proper cabinets over a five-day work week. Answer Questions 16 through 18 SOLELY upon the data provided in the graph.

16. The day during which the LARGEST number of applications was filed by both clerks was   16.___

    A. Monday   B. Tuesday   C. Wednesday   D. Friday

17. At the end of the second day, the percentage of applications STILL to be filed was   17.___

    A. 25%   B. 50%   C. 66%   D. 75%

18. Assuming that the production pattern is the same the following week as the week shown   18.___
in the chart, the day on which the file clerks will FINISH this assignment will be

    A. Monday   B. Tuesday   C. Wednesday   D. Friday

Questions 19-21.

DIRECTIONS: The following chart shows the differences between the rates of production of
employees in Department D in 1996 and 2006. Answer Questions 19 through
21 SOLELY on the basis of the information given in the chart.

Number of Employees Producing Work-Units Within Range in 1996	Number of Work-Units Produced	Number of Employees Producing Work-Units Within Range in 2006
7	500 - 1000	4
14	1001 - 1500	11
26	1501 - 2000	28
22	2001 - 2500	36
17	2501 - 3000	39
10	3001 - 3500	23
4	3501 - 4000	9

19. Assuming that within each range of work-units produced the average production was at   19.___
the mid-point at that range (e.g., category 500 - 1000 = 750), then the AVERAGE number
of work-units produced per employee in 1996 fell into the range

    A. 1001 - 1500   B. 1501 - 2000
    C. 2001 - 2500   D. 2501 - 3000

20. The ratio of the number of employees producing more than 2000 work-units in 1996 to   20.___
the number of employees producing more than 2000 work-units in 2006 is *most nearly*

    A. 1:2   B. 2:3   C. 3:4   D. 4:5

21. In Department D, which of the following were GREATER in 2006 than in 1996?   21.___
    I.   Total number of employees
    II.   Total number of work-units produced
    III.   Number of employees producing 2000 or fewer work-units
The CORRECT answer is:

    A. I, II, III   B. I, II
    C. I, III   D. II, III

22. Unit S's production fluctuated substantially from one year to another. In 2004, Unit S's production was 100% greater than in 2003. In 2005, production decreased by 25% from 2004. In 2006, Unit S's production was 10% greater than in 2005.
On the basis of this information, it is CORRECT to conclude that Unit S's production in 2006 exceeded Unit S's production in 2003 by

22._____

    A. 65%   B. 85%   C. 95%   D. 135%

23. Agency "X" is moving into a new building. It has 1500 employees presently on its staff and does not contemplate much variance from this level. The new building contains 100 available offices, each with a maximum capacity of 30 employees. It has been decided that only 2/3 of the maximum capacity of each office will be utilized. The TOTAL number of offices that will be occupied by Agency "X" is

23._____

    A. 30   B. 66   C. 75   D. 90

24. One typist completes a form letter every 5 minutes and another typist completes one every 6 minutes.
If the two typists start together, they will again start typing new letters simultaneously _____ minutes later and will have completed _____ letters by that time.

24._____

    A. 11; 30   B. 12; 24   C. 24; 12   D. 30; 11

25. During one week, a machine operator produces 10 fewer pages per hour of work than he usually does. If it ordinarily takes him six hours to produce a 300-page report, it will take him_____hours LONGER to produce that same 300-page report during the week when he produces MORE slowly.

25._____

    A. $1\frac{1}{2}$ B. $1\frac{2}{3}$ C. 2   D. $2\frac{3}{4}$

KEY (CORRECT ANSWERS)

1.	A	11.	D
2.	D	12.	C
3.	D	13.	D
4.	D	14.	C
5.	C	15.	C
6.	C	16.	C
7.	C	17.	D
8.	B	18.	B
9.	A	19.	C
10.	D	20.	A

21.	B
22.	A
23.	C
24.	D
25.	A

———

EXAMINATION SECTION
TEST 1

DIRECTIONS: Each question or incomplete statement is followed by several suggested answers or completions. Select the one that BEST answers the question or completes the statement. *PRINT THE LETTER OF THE CORRECT ANSWER IN THE SPACE AT THE RIGHT.*

1. As a supervisor in a bureau, you have been asked by the head of the bureau to recommend whether or not the work of the bureau requires an increase in the permanent staff of the bureau.
   Of the following questions, the one whose answer would MOST likely assist you in making your recommendation is: Are

   A. some permanent employees working irregular hours because they occasionally work overtime?
   B. the present permanent employees satisfied with their work assignments?
   C. temporary employees hired to handle seasonal fluctuations in work load?
   D. the present permanent employees keeping the work of the bureau current?

   1.____

2. In making job assignments to his subordinates, a supervisor should follow the principle that each individual GENERALLY is capable of

   A. performing one type of work well and less capable of performing other types well
   B. learning to perform a wide variety of different types of work
   C. performing best the type of work in which he has had experience
   D. learning to perform any type of work in which he is given training

   2.____

3. Assume that you are the supervisor of a large number of clerks in a unit in a city agency. Your unit has just been given an important assignment which must be completed a week from now. You know that, henceforth, your unit will be given this assignment every six months.
   You or any one of your subordinates who has been properly instructed can complete this assignment in one day. This assignment is of a routine type which is ordinarily handled by clerks. There is enough time for you to train one of your subordinates to handle the assignment and then have him do it. However, it would take twice as much time for you to take this course of action as it would for you to do the assignment yourself. The one of the following courses of action which you should take in this situation is to

   A. do the assignment yourself as soon as possible without discussing it with any of your subordinates at this time
   B. do the assignment yourself and then train one of your subordinates to handle it in the future
   C. give the assignment to one of your subordinates after training him to handle it
   D. train each of your subordinates to do the assignment on a rotating basis after you have done it yourself the first time

   3.____

4. You are in charge of an office in which each member of the staff has a different set of   4.___
duties, although each has the same title. No member of the staff can perform the duties
of any other member of the staff without first receiving extensive training. Assume that it
is necessary for one member of the staff to take on, in addition to his regular work, an
assignment which any member of the staff is capable of carrying out.
The one of the following considerations which would have the MOST weight in determining which staff member is to be given the additional assignment is the

    A. quality of the work performed by the individual members of the staff
    B. time consumed by individual members of the staff in performing their work
    C. level of difficulty of the duties being performed by individual members of the staff
    D. relative importance of the duties being performed by individual members of the
       staff

5. The one of the following causes of clerical error which is usually considered to be LEAST   5.___
attributable to faulty supervision or inefficient management is

    A. inability to carry out instructions
    B. too much work to do
    C. an inappropriate recordkeeping system
    D. continual interruptions

6. Suppose you are in charge of a large unit in which all of the clerical staff perform similar   6.___
tasks.
In evaluating the relative accuracy of the clerks, the clerk who should be considered to
be the LEAST accurate is the one

    A. whose errors result in the greatest financial loss
    B. whose errors cost the most to locate
    C. who makes the greatest percentage of errors in his work
    D. who makes the greatest number of errors in the unit

7. Assume that under a proposed procedure for handling employee grievances in a public   7.___
agency, the first step to be taken is for the aggrieved employee to submit his grievance as
soon as it arises to a grievance board set up to hear all employee grievances in the
agency. The board, which is to consist of representatives of management and of rank
and file employees, is to consider the grievance, obtain all necessary pertinent information, and then render a decision on the matter. Thus, the first-line supervisor would not
be involved in the settlement of any of his subordinates' grievances except when asked
by the board to submit information.
This proposed procedure would be generally UNDESIRABLE chiefly because the

    A. board may become a bottleneck to delay the prompt disposition of grievances
    B. aggrieved employees and their supervisors have not been first given the opportu-
       nity to resolve the grievances themselves
    C. employees would be likely to submit imaginary, as well as real, grievances to the
       board
    D. board will lack first-hand, personal knowledge of the factors involved in grievances

8. Sometimes jobs in private organizations and public agencies are broken down so as to   8.___
permit a high degree of job specialization.
Of the following, an IMPORTANT effect of a high degree of job specialization in a public agency is that employees performing

A. highly specialized jobs may not be readily transferable to other jobs in the agency
B. similar duties may require closer supervision than employees performing unrelated functions
C. specialized duties can be held responsible for their work to a greater extent than can employees performing a wide variety of functions
D. specialized duties will tend to cooperate readily with employees performing other types of specialized duties

9. Assume that you are the supervisor of a clerical unit in an agency. One of your subordi-   9.____
nates violates a rule of the agency, a violation which requires that the employee be sus-
pended from his work for one day. The violated rule is one that you have found to be
unduly strict, and you have recommended to the management of the agency that the rule
be changed or abolished. The management has been considering your recommendation
but has not yet reached a decision on the matter.
In these circumstances, you should

A. not initiate disciplinary action but, instead, explain to the employee that the rule may be Changed shortly
B. delay disciplinary action on the violation until the management has reached a decision on changing the rule
C. modify the disciplinary action by reprimanding the employee and informing him that further action may be taken when the management has reached a decision on changing the rule
D. initiate the prescribed disciplinary action without commenting on the strictness of the rule or on your recommendation

10. Assume that a supervisor praises his subordinates for satisfactory aspects of their work   10.____
only when he is about to criticize them for unsatisfactory aspects of their work.
Such a practice is UNDESIRABLE primarily because

A. his subordinates may expect to be praised for their work even if it is unsatisfactory
B. praising his subordinates for some aspects of their work while criticizing other aspects will weaken the effects of the criticisms
C. his subordinates would be more receptive to criticism if it were followed by praise
D. his subordinates may come to disregard praise and wait for criticism to be given

11. The one of the following which would be the BEST reason for an agency to eliminate a   11.____
procedure for obtaining and recording certain information is that

A. it is no longer legally required to obtain the information
B. there is no advantage in obtaining the information
C. the information could be compiled on the basis of other information available
D. the information obtained is sometimes incorrect

12. In determining the type and number of records to be kept in an agency, it is important to   12.____
recognize that records are of value PRIMARILY as

A. raw material to be used in statistical analysis
B. sources of information about the agency's activities
C. by-products of the activities carried on by the agency
D. data for evaluating the effectiveness of the agency

13. Aside from requirements imposed by authority, the frequency with which reports are submitted or the length of the interval which they cover should depend PRINCIPALLY on the

    A. availability of the data to be included in the reports
    B. amount of time required to prepare the reports
    C. extent of the variations in the data with the passage of time
    D. degree of comprehensiveness required in the reports

14. Organizations that occupy large, general, open-area offices sometimes consider it desirable to build private offices for the supervisors of large bureaus.
The one of the following which is generally NOT considered to be a justification of the use of private offices is that they

    A. lend prestige to the person occupying the office
    B. provide facilities for private conferences
    C. achieve the maximum use of office space
    D. provide facilities for performing work requiring a high degree of concentration

15. The LEAST important factor to be considered in planning the layout of an office is the

    A. relative importance of the different types of work to be done
    B. convenience with which communication can be achieved
    C. functional relationships of the activities of the office
    D. necessity for screening confidential activities from unauthorized persons

16. The one of the following which is generally considered to be the CHIEF advantage of using data processing equipment in modern offices is to

    A. facilitate the use of a wide variety of sources of information
    B. supply management with current information quickly
    C. provide uniformity in the processing and reporting of information
    D. broaden the area in which management decisions can be made

17. In the box design of office forms, the spaces in which information is to be entered are arranged in boxes containing captions.
Of the following, the one which is generally NOT considered to be an acceptable rule in employing box design is that

    A. space should be allowed for the lengthiest anticipated entry in a box
    B. the caption should be located in the upper left corner of the box
    C. the boxes on a form should be of the same size and shape
    D. boxes should be aligned vertically whenever possible

18. As a management tool, the work count would generally be of LEAST assistance to a unit supervisor in

    A. scheduling the work of his unit
    B. locating bottlenecks in the work of his unit
    C. ascertaining the number of subordinates he needs
    D. tracing the flow of work in the unit

19. Of the following, the FIRST step that should be taken in a forms simplification program is to make a

A. detailed analysis of the items found on current forms
B. study of the amount of use made of existing forms
C. survey of the amount of each kind of form on hand
D. survey of the characteristics of the more effective forms in use

20. The work-distribution chart is a valuable tool for an office supervisor to use in conducting   20.____
work'simplification programs.
Of the following questions, the one which a work-distribution chart would generally be
LEAST useful in answering is:

A. What activities take the most time?
B. Are the employees doing many unrelated tasks?
C. Is work being distributed evenly among the employees?
D. Are activities being performed in proper sequence?

21. Assume that, as a supervisor, you conduct, from time to time, work-performance studies   21.____
in various sections of your agency. The units of measurement used in any study depend
on the particular study and may be number of letters typed, number of papers filed, or
other suitable units.
It is MOST important that the units of measurement to be used in a study conform to
the units used in similar past studies when the

A. units of measurement to be used in the study cannot be defined sharply
B. units of measurement used in past studies were satisfactory
C. results of the study are to be compared with those of past studies
D. results of the study are to be used for the same purpose as were those of past
studies

22. As it is used in auditing, an internal check is a   22.____

A. procedure which is designed to guard against fraud
B. periodic audit by a public accounting firm to verify the accuracy of the internal
transactions of an organization
C. document transferring funds from one section to another within an organization
D. practice of checking documents twice before they are transmitted outside an orga-
nization

23. Of the following, the one which can LEAST be considered to be a proper function of an   23.____
accounting system is to

A. indicate the need to curtail expenditures
B. provide information for future fiscal programs
C. record the expenditure of funds from special appropriations
D. suggest methods to expedite the collection of revenues

24. Assume that a new unit is to be established in an agency. The unit is to compile and tab-   24.____
ulate data so that it will be of the greatest usefulness to the high-level administrators in
the agency in making administrative decisions. In planning the organization of this unit,
the question that should be answered FIRST is:

A. What interpretations are likely to be made of the data by the high-level administrators in making decisions?
B. At what point in the decision-making process will it be most useful to inject the data?
C. What types of data will be required by high-level administrators in making decisions?
D. What criteria will the high-level administrators use to evaluate the decisions they make?

25. The one of the following which is the CHIEF limitation of the organization chart as it is generally used in business and government is that the chart   25.___

    A. engenders within incumbents feelings of rights to positions they occupy
    B. reveals only formal authority relationships, omitting the informal ones
    C. shows varying degrees of authority even though authority is not subject to such differentiation
    D. presents organizational structure as it is rather than what it is supposed to be

26. The degree of decentralization that is effective and economical in an organization tends to vary INVERSELY with the   26.___

    A. size of the organization
    B. availability of adequate numbers of competent personnel
    C. physical dispersion of the organization's activities
    D. adequacy of the organization's communications system

27. The one of the following which usually can LEAST be considered to be an advantage of committees as they are generally used in government and business is that they   27.___

    A. provide opportunities for reconciling varying points of view
    B. promote coordination by the interchange of information among the members of the committee
    C. act promptly in situations requiring immediate action
    D. use group judgment to resolve questions requiring a wide range of experience

28. Managerial decentralization is defined as the decentralization of decision-making authority.
    The degree of managerial decentralization in an organization varies INVERSELY with the   28.___

    A. number of decisions made lower down the management hierarchy
    B. importance of the decisions made lower down the management hierarchy
    C. number of major organizational functions affected by decisions made at lower management levels
    D. amount of review to which decisions made at lower management levels are subjected

29. Some policy-making commissions are composed of members who are appointed to overlapping terms.
    Of the following, the CHIEF advantage of appointing members to overlapping terms in such commissions is that   29.___

A. continuity of policy is promoted
B. the likelihood of compromise policy decisions is reduced
C. responsibility for policy decisions can be fixed upon individual members
D. the likelihood of unanimity of opinion is increased

30. If a certain public agency with a fixed number of employees has a line organizational structure, then the width of the span of supervision is   30._____

A. inversely proportional to the length of the chain of command in the organization
B. directly proportional to the complexity of tasks performed in the organization
C. inversely proportional to the competence of the personnel in the organization
D. directly proportional to the number of levels of supervision existing in the organization

31. Mr. Brown is a supervisor in charge of a section of clerical employees in an agency. The   31._____ section consists of four units, each headed by a unit supervisor. From time to time, he makes tours of his section for the purpose of maintaining contact with the rank and file employees. During these tours, he discusses with these employees their work production, work methods, work problems, and other related topics. The information he obtains in this manner is often incomplete or inaccurate. At meetings with the unit supervisors, he questions them on the information acquired during his tours. The supervisors are often unable to answer the questions immediately because they are based on incomplete or inaccurate information. When the supervisors ask that they be permitted to accompany Mr. Brown on his tours and thus answer his questions on the spot, Mr. Brown refuses, explaining that a rank and file employee might be reluctant to speak freely in the presence of his supervisor. This situation may BEST be described as a violation of the principle of organization called

A. span of control
C. specialization of work
B. delegation of authority
D. unity of command

Questions 32-36.

DIRECTIONS: Each of Questions 32 through 36 consists of a statement which contains one word that is incorrectly used because it is not in keeping with the meaning that the quotation is evidently intended to convey. For each of these questions, you are to select the INCORRECTLY used word and substitute for it one of the words lettered A, B, C, or D, which helps BEST to convey the meaning of the statement.

32. There has developed in recent years an increasing awareness of the need to measure   32._____ the quality of management in all enterprises and to seek the principles that can serve as a basis for this improvement.

A. growth   B. raise   C. efficiency   D. define

33. It is hardly an exaggeration to deny that the permanence, productivity, and humanity of   33._____ any industrial system depend upon its ability to utilize the positive and constructive impulses of all who work and upon its ability to arouse and continue interest in the necessary activities.

A. develop
C. state
B. efficiency
D. inspirational

34. The selection of managers on the basis of technical knowledge alone seems to recognize that the essential characteristic of management is getting things done through others, thereby demanding skills that are essential in coordinating the activities of subordinates.

    A. training   B. fails
    C. organization   D. improving

35. Only when it is deliberate and when it is clearly understood what impressions the ease of communication will probably create in the minds of employees and subordinate management, should top management refrain from commenting on a subject that is of general concern.

    A. obvious   B. benefit   C. doubt   D. absence

36. Scientific planning of work requires careful analysis of facts and a precise plan of action for the whims and fancies of executives that often provide only a vague indication of the work to be done.

    A. substitutes   B. development
    C. preliminary   D. comprehensive

37. Within any single level of government, as a city or a state, the administrative authority may be concentrated or dispersed.
Of the following plans of government, the one in which administrative authority would be dispersed the MOST is the _____ plan.

    A. mayor   B. mayor-council
    C. commission   D. city manager

38. In general, the courts may review a decision of an administrative agency with rule-making powers. However, the courts will usually REFUSE to review a decision of such an agency if the only question raised concerning the decision is whether or not the

    A. decision contravenes public policy
    B. agency has abused the powers conferred upon it
    C. decision deals with an issue which is within the jurisdiction of the agency
    D. agency has applied the same rules of evidence as are used in the courts

39. A legislature sometimes delegates rule-making powers to the administrators of a public agency.
Of the following, the CHIEF advantage of such delegation is that

    A. the frequency with which the legality of the agency's rules is contested in court will be reduced
    B. the agency will have the flexibility to adjust to changing conditions and problems
    C. mistakes made by the administrators or the legislature in defining the scope of the agency's program may be easily corrected
    D. the legislature will not be required to approve the rules formulated by the agency

40. Some municipalities have delegated the functions of budget preparation and personnel selection to central agencies, thus removing these functions from operating departments.
Of the following, the MOST important reason why municipalities have delegated these functions to central agencies is that

A. the performance of these functions presents problems that vary from one operating department to another
B. operating departments often lack sufficient funds to perform these functions adequately
C. the performance of these functions by a central agency produces more uniform policies than if these functions are performed by the operating departments
D. central agencies are not controlled as closely as are operating departments and so have greater freedom in formulating new policies and procedures to deal with difficult budget and personnel problems

41. Of the following, the MOST fundamental reason for the use of budgets in governmental administration is that budgets

41.____

A. minimize seasonal variations in work loads and expenditures of public agencies
B. facilitate decentralization of functions performed by public agencies
C. provide advance control on the expenditure of funds
D. establish valid bases for comparing present governmental activities with corresponding activities in previous periods

42. In some governmental jurisdictions, the chief executive prepares the budget for a fiscal period and presents it to the legislative branch of government for adoption. In other jurisdictions, the legislative branch prepares and adopts the budget.
Preparation of the budget by the chief executive rather than by the legislative branch is

42.____

A. *desirable*, primarily because the chief executive is held largely accountable by the public for the results of fiscal operations and should, therefore, be the one to prepare the budget
B. *undesirable*, primarily because such a separation of the legislative and executive branches leads to the enactment of a budget that does not consider the overall needs of the government
C. *desirable*, primarily because the preparation of the budget by the chief executive limits legislative review and evaluation of operating programs
D. *undesirable*, primarily because responsibility for budget preparation should be placed in the branch that must eventually adopt the budget and appropriate the funds for it

43. The one of the following which is generally the FIRST step in the budget-making process of a municipality that has a central budget agency is

43.____

A. determination of available sources of revenue within the municipality
B. establishment of tax rates at levels sufficient to achieve a balanced budget in the following fiscal period
C. evaluation by the central budget agency of the adequacy of the municipality's previous budgets
D. assembling by the central budget agency of the proposed expenditures of each agency in the municipality for the following fiscal period

44. It is advantageous for a municipality to issue serial bonds rather than sinking fund bonds CHIEFLY because

44.____

A. an issue of serial bonds usually includes a wider range of maturity dates than does an issue of sinking fund bonds
B. appropriations set aside periodically to retire serial bonds as they fall due are more readily invested in long-term securities at favorable rates of interest than are appropriations earmarked for redemption of sinking fund bonds
C. serial bonds are sold at regular intervals while sinking fund bonds are issued as the need for funds arises
D. a greater variety of interest rates is usually offered in an issue of serial bonds than in an issue of sinking fund bonds

45. Studies conducted by the Regional Plan Association of the 22-county New York Metropolitan Region, comprising New York City and surrounding counties in New York, New Jersey, and Connecticut, have defined Manhattan, Brooklyn, Queens, the Bronx, and Hudson County in New Jersey as the *core.* Such studies have examined the per capita personal income of the core as a percent of the per capita personal income of the entire Region, and the population of the core as a percent of the total population of the entire Region.
These studies support the conclusion that, as a percent of the entire Region,

45.___

A. both population and per capita personal income in the core were higher in 1970 than in 1940
B. both population and per capita personal income in the core were lower in 1970 than in 1940
C. population was higher and per capita personal income was lower in the core in 1970 than in 1940
D. population was lower and per capita personal income was higher in the core in 1970 than in 1940

KEY (CORRECT ANSWERS)

1. D	11. B	21. C	31. D	41. C
2. B	12. B	22. A	32. B	42. A
3. C	13. C	23. D	33. C	43. D
4. B	14. C	24. C	34. B	44. A
5. A	15. A	25. B	35. D	45. B
6. C	16. B	26. D	36. A	
7. B	17. C	27. C	37. C	
8. A	18. D	28. D	38. D	
9. D	19. B	29. A	39. B	
10. D	20. D	30. A	40. C	

EXAMINATION SECTION

DIRECTIONS FOR THIS SECTION:
Each question or incomplete statement is followed by several suggested answers or completions. Select the one that BEST answers the question or completes the statement. *PRINT THE LETTER OF THE CORRECT ANSWER IN THE SPACE AT THE RIGHT.*

TEST 1

1. A supervisor notices that one of his more competent subordinates has recently been showing less interest in his work. The work performed by this employee has also fallen off and he seems to want to do no more than the minimum acceptable amount of work. When his supervisor questions the subordinate about his decreased interest and his mediocre work performance, the subordinates replies: "Sure, I've lost interest in my work. I don't see any reason why I should do more than I have to. When I do a good job, nobody notices it. But, let me fall down on one minor job and the whole place knows about it! So why should I put myself out on this job?"
If the subordinate's contentions are true, it would be CORRECT to *assume* that the
   A. subordinate has not received adequate training
   B. subordinate's workload should be decreased
   C. supervisor must share responsibility for this employee's reaction
   D. supervisor has not been properly enforcing work standards

2. How many subordinates should report directly to each supervisor? While there is agreement that there are limits to the number of subordinates that a manager can supervise well, this limit is determined by a number of important factors.
Which of the following factors is *most likely* to increase the number of subordinates that can be EFFECTIVELY supervised by one supervisor in a particular unit?
   A. The unit has a great variety of activities.
   B. A staff assistant handles the supervisor's routine duties.
   C. The unit has a relatively inexperienced staff.
   D. The office layout is being rearranged to make room for more employees.

3. Mary Smith, an administrative assistant, heads the inspection records unit of Department Y. She is a dedicated supervisor who not only strives to maintain an efficient operation, but also tries to improve the competence of each individual member of her staff. She keeps these considerations in mind when assigning work to her staff. Her bureau chief asks her to compile some data based on information contained in her records. She feels that any member of her staff should be able to do this job.
The one of the following members of her staff who would *probably* be given LEAST consideration for this assignment is:
   A. Jane Abel, a capable supervising clerk with considerable experience in the unit
   B. Kenneth Brown, a senior clerk recently transferred to

1. ...

2. ...

3. ...

1

the unit, who has had several opportunities to demonstrate his capabilities

    C. Laura Chance, a clerk who spends full time on a single routine assignment

    D. Michael Dutton, a clerk who works on several minor jobs but still has the lightest work load

4. There are very few aspects of a supervisor's job that do not involve communication, either in writing or orally. Which of the following statements regarding *oral* and *written* orders is NOT correct?   4. ...

    A. Oral orders usually permit more immediate feedback than do written orders.

    B. Written orders, rather than oral orders, should generally be given when the subordinate will be held strictly accountable.

    C. Oral orders are usually preferable when the order contains lengthy detailed instructions.

    D. Written orders, rather than oral orders, should usually be given to a subordinate who is slow to understand or is forgetful.

5. Assume that you are the head of a large clerical unit in Department R. Your department's personnel office has appointed a clerk, Roberta Rowe, to fill a vacancy in your unit. Before bringing this appointee to your office, the personnel officer has given Roberta the standard orientation on salary, fringe benefits, working conditions, attendance, and the department's personnel rules. In addition, he has supplied her with literature covering these areas. Of the following, the action that you should take FIRST after Roberta has been brought to your office is to   5. ...

    A. give her an opportunity to read the literature furnished by the personnel office so that she can ask you questions about it

    B. escort her to the desk she will use and assign her to work with an experienced employee who will act as her trainer

    C. explain the duties and responsibilities of her job and its relationship with the jobs being performed by the other employees of the unit

    D. summon the employee who is currently doing the work that will be performed by Roberta and have him explain and demonstrate how to perform the required tasks

6. Your superior informs you that the employee turnover rate in your office is well above the norm and must be reduced. Which one of the following initial steps would be LEAST appropriate in attempting to overcome this problem?   6. ...

    A. Decide to be more lenient about performance standards and about employee requests for time off, so that your office will gain a reputation as an easy place to work

    B. Discuss the problem with a few of your key people whose judgment you trust to see if they can shed some light on the underlying causes of the problem

    C. Review the records of employees who have left during the past year to see if there is a pattern that will help you understand the problem

    D. Carefully review your training procedures to see
       whether they can be improved

7. In issuing instructions to a subordinate on a job assign-   7. ...
ment, the supervisor should ordinarily explain why the
assignment is being made.
Omission of such an explanation is BEST justified when the
    A. subordinate is restricted in the amount of discretion
       he can exercise in carrying out the assignment
    B. assignment is one that will be unpopular with the
       subordinate
    C. subordinate understands the reason as a result of
       previous similar assignments
    D. assignment is given to an employee who is in need of
       further training

8. When a supervisor allows sufficient time for training and   8. ...
makes an appropriate effort in the training of his subordinates, his CHIEF goal is to
    A. increase the dependence of one subordinate upon
       another in their everyday work activities
    B. spend more time with his subordinates in order to
       become more involved in their work'
    C. increase the capability and independence of his
       subordinates in carrying out their work
    D. increase his frequency of contact with his subordi-
       nates in order to better evaluate their performance

9. In preparing an evaluation of a subordinate's performance,   9. ...
which one of the following items is *usually* IRRELEVANT?
    A. Remarks about tardiness or absenteeism
    B. Mention of any unusual contributions or accomplishments
    C. A summary of the employee's previous job experience
    D. An assessment of the employee's attitude toward the job

10. The ability to delegate responsibility while maintaining   10. ...
adequate controls is one key to a supervisor's success.
Which one of the following methods of control would MINI-
MIZE the amount of responsibility assumed by the subordinate?
    A. Asking for a monthly status report in writing
    B. Asking to receive copies of important correspondence so
       that you can be aware of potential problems
    C. Scheduling periodic project status conferences with
       your subordinate
    D. Requiring that your subordinate confer with you before
       making decisions on a project

11. You wish to assign an important project to a subordinate   11. ...
who you think has good potential.
Which one of the following approaches would be MOST effective in successfully completing the project while developing the subordinate's abilities?
    A. Describe the project to the subordinate in general
       terms and emphasize that it must be completed as
       quickly as possible
    B. Outline the project in detail to the subordinate and
       emphasize that its successful completion could lead
       to career advancement
    C. Develop a detailed project outline and timetable,
       discuss the details and timing with him, and assign
       the subordinate to carry out the plan on his own

3

    D. Discuss the project objectives and suggested approaches
       with the subordinate, and ask the subordinate to develop
       a detailed project outline and timetable for your ap-
       proval

12. Research studies reveal that an important difference be-   12. ...
    tween high-production and low-production supervisors lies
    not in their interest in eliminating mistakes, but in their
    manner of handling mistakes.
    High-production supervisors are *most likely* to look upon
    mistakes as PRIMARILY a(n)
      A. opportunity to provide training
      B. by-product of subordinate negligence
      C. opportunity to fix blame in a situation
      D. result of their own incompetence

13. Supervisors should try to establish what has been called   13. ...
    "positive discipline," an atmosphere in which subordinates
    willingly abide by rules which they consider fair.
    When a supervisor notices a subordinate violating an im-
    portant rule, his FIRST course of action should be to
      A. stop the subordinate and tell him what he is doing wrong
      B. wait a day or two before approaching the employee in-
        volved
      C. call a meeting of all subordinates to discuss the rule
      D. forget the matter in the hope that it will not happen
        again

14. The working climate is the feeling, degree of freedom, the 14. ...
    tone and the mood of the working environment.
    Which of the following contributes MOST to determining the
    working climate in a unit or group? The
      A. rules set for rest periods
      B. example set by the supervisor
      C. rules set for morning check in
      D. wages paid to the employees

15. John Polk is a bright, ingenious clerk with a lot of   15. ...
    initiative. He has made many good suggestions to his
    supervisor in the training division of Department T, where
    he is employed. However, last week one of his bright ideas
    literally "blew up." In setting up some electronic equip-
    ment in the training classroom, he crossed some wires, re-
    sulting in a damaged tape recorder and a classroom so filled
    with smoke that the training class had to be held in another
    room. When Mr. Brown, his supervisor, learned of this oc-
    currence, he immediately summoned John to his private office.
    There Mr. Brown spent five minutes bawling John out, calling
    him an over-zealous, overgrown kid, and sent him back to his
    job without letting John speak once.
    Of the following, the action of Mr. Brown that MOST deserves
    approval is that he
      A. took disciplinary action immediately without regard
        for past performance
      B. kept the disciplinary interview to a brief period
      C. concentrated his criticism on the root cause of the
        occurrence
      D. held the disciplinary interview in his private office

16. Typically, when the technique of "supervision by results" 16. ...
    is practiced, higher management sets down, either implicitly or

4

explicitly, certain performance standards or goals that the subordinate is expected to meet. So long as these standards are met, management interferes very little.

The *most likely* result of the use of this technique is that it will

 A. lead to ambiguity in terms of goals

 B. be successful only to the extent that close direct supervision is practiced

 C. make it possible to evaluate both employee and supervisory effectiveness

 D. allow for complete automomy on the subordinate's part

17. Assume that you are the supervisor of a large clerical   17. ...
unit performing routine clerical operations. One of your clerks consistenly produces much less work than other members of your staff performing similar tasks.

Of the following, the action you should take FIRST is to

 A. ask the clerk if he wants to be transferred to another unit

 B. reprimand the clerk for his poor performance and warn him that further disciplinary action will be taken if his work does not improve

 C. quietly ask the clerk's co-workers whether they know why his performance is poor

 D. discuss this matter with the clerk to work out plans for improving his performance

18. When making written evaluations and reviews of the per-   18. ...
formance of subordinates, it is *usually* advisable to

 A. avoid informing the employee of the evaluation if it is critical because it may create hard feelings

 B. avoid informing the employee of the evaluation whether critical or favorable because it is tension-producing

 C. to permit the employee to see the evaluation but not to discuss it with him because the supervisor cannot be certain where the discussion might lead

 D. to discuss the evaluation openly with the employee because it helps the employee understand what is expected of him

19. There are a number of well-known and respected human re-   19. ...
lations principles that successful supervisors have been using for years in building good relationships with their employees.

Which of the following does NOT illustrate such a principle?

 A. Give clear and complete instructions

 B. Let each person know how he is getting along

 C. Keep an open-door policy

 D. Make all relationships personal ones

20. Assume that it is your responsibility to maintain certain   20. ...
personnel records that are continually being updated. You have three senior clerks assigned specifically to this task. Recently you have noticed that the volume of work has increased substantially, and the processing of personnel records by the clerks is backlogged. Your supervisor is now receiving complaints due to the processing delay.

Of the following, the *best* course of action for you to take FIRST is to

A. have a meeting with the clerks, advise them of the problem, and ask that they do their work faster; then confirm your meeting in writing for the record

B. request that an additional position be authorized for your unit

C. review the procedures being used for processing the work, and try to determine if you can improve the flow of work

D. get the system moving faster by spending some of your own time processing the backlog

21. Assume that you are in charge of a payroll unit consisting 21. ... of four clerks. It is Friday, November 14. You have just arrived in the office after a conference. Your staff is preparing a payroll that must be forwarded the following Monday.
Which of the following new items on your desk should you attend to FIRST? A

   A. telephone message regarding very important information needed for the statistical summary of salaries paid for the month of November

   B. memorandum regarding a new procedure that should be followed in preparing the payroll

   C. telephone message from an employee who is threatening to endorse his pay check "Under Protest" because he is dissatisfied with the amount

   D. memorandum from your supervisor reminding you to submit the probationary period report on a new employee

22. You are in charge of a unit that orders and issues sup- 22. ... plies. On a particular day you are faced with the following four situations. Which one should you take care of FIRST?

   A. One of your employees who is in the process of taking the quarterly inventory of supplies has telephoned and asked that you return his call as soon as possible.

   B. A representative of a company that is noted for producing excellent office supplies will soon arrive with samples for you to distribute to the various offices in your agency.

   C. A large order of supplies which was delivered this morning has been checked and counted and a deliveryman is waiting for you to sign the receipt.

   D. A clerk from the purchase division asks you to search for a bill you failed to send to them which is urgently needed in order for them to complete a report due this morning.

23. Assume that it is necessary for you to give an unpleasant 23. ... assignment to one of your subordinates. You expect this employee to raise some objections to this assignment.
The *most appropriate* of the following actions for you to take FIRST is to issue the assignment

   A. orally, with the further statement that you will not listen to any complaints

   B. in writing, to forestall any complaints by the employee

   C. orally, permitting the employee to express his feelings

   D. in writing, with a note that any comments should be submitted in writing

24. Your office has recently acquired its own electrostatic   24. ...
copier. During the first two months of use, copying costs
have greatly exceeded the budgeted amount, and you have
been asked to take steps to reduce this cost.
Which one of the following steps would be LEAST effective
in solving this problem?
   A. Making sure that employees use carbons, rather than
the copier, for file copies of ordinary correspondence
   B. Turning off the copier for two hours each day
   C. Analyzing the need for copies of routine reports, and
eliminating useless copies
   D. Requiring that a different copying process, such as
memeograph, be used when large numbers of copies are
needed

25. A Centrex telephone system allows both incoming and outgo- 25. ...
ing calls to be completed directly without going through a
switchboard operator. An outside caller can reach a particular employee by direct dialing.
For which one of the following types of offices would this
system be MOST desirable? A(n)
   A. office dealing chiefly with complaints from tenants
   B. office whose primary function is to maintain accounting records
   C. office that receives and processes applications for
certain kinds of permits
   D. purchasing office where each employee maintains contact with a number of regular suppliers

TEST 2

1. Cycling is an arrangement where papers are processed   1. ...
throughout a period according to an orderly plan rather
than as a group all at one time. This technique has been
used for a long time by public utilities in their cycle
billing.
Of the following practices, the one that BEST illustrates
this technique is that in which
   A. paychecks for per annum employees are issued bi-weekly
and those for per diem employees are issued weekly
   B. field inspectors report in person to their offices one
day a week, on Fridays, when they do all their paper-
work and also pick up their paychecks
   C. the dates for issuing relief checks to clients vary
depending on the last digit of the clients' social
security numbers
   D. the last day for filing and paying income taxes is
the same for Federal, State, and City income taxes

2. The employees in your division have recently been given   2. ...
an excellent up-to-date office manual, but you find that
a good number of employees are not following the procedures
outlined in it.
Which one of the following would be *most likely* to ensure
that employees begin using the manual EFFECTIVELY?
   A. Require each employee to keep a copy of the manual
in plain sight on his desk

    B. Issue warnings periodically to those employees who
       deviate most from procedures prescribed in the manual
    C. Tell an employee to check his manual when he does not
       follow the proper procedures
    D. Suggest to the employees that the manual be studied
       thoroughly

3. The one of the following factors which should be considered 3. ...
FIRST in the design of office forms is the
    A. information to be included in the form
    B. sequence of the information
    C. purpose of the form
    D. persons who will be using the form

4. Window envelopes are being used to an increasing extent by 4. ...
government and private industry.
The *one* of the following that is NOT an advantage of window
envelopes is that they
    A. cut down on addressing costs
    B. eliminate the need to attach envelopes to letters being
       sent forward for signature by a superior
    C. are less costly to buy than regular envelopes
    D. reduce the risk of having letters placed in wrong
       envelopes

5. Your bureau's typing unit is getting bogged down with work. 5. ...
Your bureau head wants you to look into this problem. You
find that much time is spent by the typists in inserting
and then removing carbons used in preparing form notices
in quadruplicate. The carbon copies are kept by the units
to which they are routed for a maximum of two years. You
suggest, as a time-saver, that these notices be printed as
4-part carbon interleaved sets.
In selecting the paper to be used for these 4-part carbon
interleaved forms, you would find it MOST desirable to use
    A. 16-lb., 100% rag content paper
    B. 16-lb., 100% sulphite paper
    C. 20-lb., 25% rag content paper D. 20-lb., ledger paper

6. Your bureau head asks you to prepare the office layouts for 6. ...
several of his units being moved to a higher floor in your
office building.
Of the following possibilities, the *one* that you should
AVOID in preparing the layouts is to
    A. place the desks of the first-line supervisors near
       those of the staffs they supervise
    B. place the desks of employees whose work is most close-
       ly related near one another
    C. arrange the desks so that employees do not face one
       another
    D. locate desks with many outside visitors farthest from
       the office entrance

7. Which one of the following conditions would be LEAST impor- 7. ...
tant in considering a change of the layout in a particular
office?
    A. Installation of a new office machine
    B. Assignment of five additional employees to your office
    C. Poor flow of work
    D. Employees' personal preferences of desk location

8

8. Your bureau head asks you to design an application form   8. ...
that will be filled out either in handwriting or by type-
writer. The information supplied on this form will be keypunched for subsequent processing on a computer. In designing this form, you intend to make it as easy as possible
for the keypunch operator to transcribe the information that
is to be keypunched.
The *one* of the following considerations that will contribute
LEAST to carrying out this intention is the
    A. color of the ink to be used in printing the form
    B. similarity in sequence of items on the form and the
       key punch card
    C. size of the type to be used in printing the form
    D. substance and weight of the paper used for the form

9. Which of the following duplicating processes should be   9. ...
used to make 10,000 copies of a letter-sized form?
    A. Photo-offset process   B. Xerox process
    C. Mimeograph process   D. Spirit duplicating process

10. Suppose Mr. Blount, an administrative assistant, is dic-   10. ...
tating a letter to a stenographer. His dictation begins
with the name of the addressee and continues to the body
of the letter. However, Mr. Blount does not dictate the
address of the recipient of the letter. He expects the
stenographer to locate it.
The use of this practice by Mr. Blount is
    A. *acceptable*, especially if he gives the stenographer
       the letter to which he is responding
    B. *acceptable*, especially if the letter is lengthy and
       detailed
    C. *unacceptable*, because it is not part of a steno-
       rapher's duties to search for information
    D. *unacceptable*, because he should not rely on the ac-
       curacy of the stenographer

11. Assume that there are no rules, directives, or instruc-   11. ...
tions concerning the filing of materials in your office
or the retention of such files. A system is now being
followed of placing in "inactive" files any materials
that are more than one year old.
Of the following, the MOST appropriate thing to do with
material that has been in an "inactive" file in your office for over one year is to
    A. inspect the contents of the files to decide how to
       dispose of them
    B. transfer the material to a nearby location, where it
       can be obtained if necessary
    C. keep the material intact for a minimum of another
       three years
    D. destroy the material which has not been needed for
       at least a year

12. Suppose you have just returned to your desk after engag-   12. ...
ing in an all-morning conference. Joe Brent, a clerk,
informs you that Clara McCloud, an administrator in another
agency, telephoned during the morning and that, although
she requested to speak with you, he was able to give her
the desired information.

Of the following, the MOST appropriate action for you to
take in regard to Mr. Brent's action is to
  A. thank him for assisting Ms. McCloud in your absence
  B. explain to him the proper telephone practice to use
     in the future
  C. reprimand him for not properly channeling Ms. McCloud's
     call
  D. issue a memo to all clerical employees regarding proper
     telephone practices

13. When interviewing subordinates with problems, supervisors   13. ...
    frequently find that asking direct questions of the em-
    ployee results only in evasive responses. The supervisor
    may, therefore, resort to the "non-directive" interview
    technique. In this technique the supervisor avoids pointed
    questions; he leads the employee to continue talking freely
    uninfluenced by the supervisor's preconceived notions.
    This technique often enables the employee to bring his prob-
    lem into sharp focus and to reach a solution to his problem.
    Suppose that you are a supervisor interviewing a subordinate
    about his recent poor attendance record. On calling his at-
    tention to his excessive lateness record, he replies: "I just
    don't seem to be able to get up in the morning. Frankly,
    I've lost interest in this job. I don't care about it. When
    I get up in the morning, I have to skip breakfast and I'm
    still late. I don't care about this job."
    If you are using the "non-directive" technique in this inter-
    view, the *most appropriate* of the following responses for
    you to make is:
      A. "You don't care about this job?"
      B. "Don't you think you are letting your department down?"
      C. "Are you having trouble at home?"
      D. "Don't you realize your actions are childish?"

Questions 14-18.
DIRECTIONS: Questions 14 through 18 are to be answered SOLELY on the
             basis of the following passage.
    General supervision, in contrast to close supervision, involves a
high degree of delegation of authority and requires some indirect
means to insure that employee behavior conforms to management needs.
Not everyone works well under general supervision, however. General
supervision works best where subordinates desire responsibility.
General supervision also works well where individuals in work groups
have strong feelings about the quality of the finished work products.
Strong identification with management goals is another trait of persons who work well under general supervision. There are substantial
differences in the amount of responsibility people are willing to ac-
dept on the job. One person may flourish under supervision that another might find extremely restrictive.
    Psychological research provides evidence that the nature of a per-
son's personality affects his attitude toward supervision. There are
some employees with a low need for achievement and high fear of failure
who shy away from challenges and responsibilities. Many seek self-
expression off the job and ask only to be allowed to daydream on it.
There are others who have become so accustomed to the authoritarian
approach in their culture, family, and previous work experience that
they regard general supervision as no supervision at all. They abuse
the privileges it bestows on them and refuse to accept the responsibilities it demands.

Different groups develop different attitudes toward work. Most college graduates, for example, expect a great deal of responsibility and freedom. People with limited education, on the other hand, often have trouble accepting the concept that people should make decisions for themselves, particularly decisions concerning work. Therefore, the extent to which general supervision will be effective varies greatly with the subordinates involved.

14. According to the above passage, which one of the following 14. ...
    is a NECESSARY part of management policy regarding general
    supervision?
       A. Most employees should formulate their own work goals.
       B. Deserving employees should be rewarded periodically.
       C. Some controls on employee work patterns should be
          established.
       D. Responsibility among employees should generally be
          equalized.

15. It can be inferred from the above passage that an employee 15. ...
    who avoids responsibilities and challenges is *most likely*
    to
       A. gain independence under general supervision
       B. work better under close supervision than under
          general supervision
       C. abuse the liberal guidelines of general supervision
       D. become more restricted and cautious under general
          supervision

16. Based on the above passage, employees who succeed under   16. ...
    general supervision are *most likely* to
       A. have a strong identification with people and their
          problems
       B. accept work obligations without fear
       C. seek self-expression off the job
       D. value the intellectual aspects of life

17. Of the following, the BEST title for the passage is: 17. ...
       A. Benefits and Disadvantages of General Supervision
       B. Production Levels of Employees under General Supervision
       C. Employee Attitudes Toward Work and the Work Environment
       D. Employee Background and Personality as a Factor in
          Utilizing General Supervision

18. It can be inferred from the above passage that the one of   18. ...
    the following employees who is *most likely* to work BEST
    under general supervision is one who
       A. is a part-time graduate student
       B. was raised by very strict parents
       C. has little self-confidence
       D. has been closely supervised in past jobs

19. An employee in a work group made the following comment to   19. ...
    a co-worker: "It's great to be a lowly employee instead
    of an administrative assistant because you can work with-
    out thinking. The administrative assistant is getting paid
    to plan, schedule, and think. Let him see to it that you
    have a productive day."
    Which one of the following statements about this statement
    BEST reflects an understanding of good personnel management
    techniques and the role of the supervising administrative
    assistant? The employee is

11

A. *wrong* in attitude and in his perception of the role of the administrative assistant
B. *correct* in attitude but is *wrong* in his perception of the role of the administrative assistant
C. *correct* in attitude and in his perception of the role of the administrative assistant
D. *wrong* in attitude but is *right* in his perception of the role of the administrative assistant

20. An administrative assistant has been criticized for the low productivity in the group which he supervises. Which of the following BEST reflects an understanding of supervisory responsibilities in the area of productivity? An administrative assistant should be held responsible for his own 20. ...

    A. individual productivity and the productivity of the group he supervises, because he is in a position where he maintains or increases production through others
    B. personal productivity only, because the supervisor is not likely to have any effect on the productivity of subordinates
    C. individual productivity but only for a drop in the productivity of the group he supervises, since subordinates will receive credit for increased productivity individually
    D. personal productivity only, because this is how he would be evaluated if he were not a supervisor

21. A supervisor has held a meeting in his office with an employee about the employee's grievance. The grievance concerned the sharp way in which the supervisor reprimanded the employee for an error the employee made in the performance of a task assigned to him. The problem was not resolved. Which one of the following statements about this meeting BEST reflects an understanding of good supervisory techniques? 21. ...

    A. It is awkward for a supervisor to handle a grievance involving himself. The supervisor should not have held the meeting.
    B. It would have been better if the supervisor had held the meeting at the employee's workplace, even though there would have been frequent distractions, because the employee would have been more relaxed.
    C. The resolution of a problem is not the only sign of a successful meeting. The achievement of communication was worthwhile.
    D. The supervisor should have been forceful. There is nothing wrong with raising your voice to an employee every once in a while.

22. John Hart, the owner of a single family house, complains that he submitted an application for reduction of assessment that obviously was not acted upon before his final assessment notice was sent to him. The timely receipt of the application has been verified in a departmental log book. As the supervisor of the clerical unit through which this application was processed and where this delay occurred, you should be LEAST concerned with 22. ...

12

A. what happened B. who is responsible
C. why it happened D. what can be learned from it

23. The one of the following that applies MOST appropriately   23. ...
to the role of the first-line supervisor is that *usually*
he is
A. called upon to help determine agency policy
B. involved in long-range agency planning
C. responsible for determining some aspects of basic
organization structure
D. a participant in developing procedures and methods

24. Sally Jones, an administrative assistant, gives clear and   24. ...
precise instructions to Robert Warren, a senior clerk. In
these instructions, Ms. Jones clearly delegates authority
to Mr. Warren to undertake a well-defined task.
In this situation Ms. Jones should expect Mr. Warren to
A. come to her to check out details as he progresses
with the task
B. come to her only with exceptional problems
C. ask her permission if he wishes to use his delegated
authority
D. use his authority to re-define the task and its related activities

25. Planning involves establishing department goals and   25. ...
programs and determining ways of reaching them.
The MAIN advantage of such planning is that
A. there will be no need for adjustments once a plan
is put into operation
B. it insures that everyone is working on schedule
C. it provides the framework for an effective operation
D. unexpected work problems are easily overcome

TEST 3

1. As a result of reorganization, the jobs in a large cleri-   1. ...
cal unit were broken down into highly specialized tasks.
Each specialized task was then assigned to a particular
employee to perform.
This action will *probably* lead to an INCREASE in
A. flexibility B. job satisfaction
C. need for coordination D. employee initiative

2. Your office carries on a large volume of correspondence   2. ...
concerned with the purchase of supplies and equipment for
city offices. You use form letters to deal with many common situations.
In which one of the following situations would use of a
form letter be LEAST appropriate?
A. Informing suppliers of a change in city regulations
concerning purchase contracts
B. Telling a new supplier the standard procedures to be
followed in billing
C. Acknowledging receipt of a complaint and saying that
the complaint will be investigated
D. Answering a city councilman's request for additional
information on a particular regulation affecting suppliers

13

3. Assume that you head a large clerical unit. Because of the great demands being made on your time, you have designated Tom Smith, a supervising clerk, to be your assistant and to assume some of your duties.
   Of the following duties performed by you, the *most appropriate* one to assign to Tom Smith is to
   A. conduct the on-the-job training of new employees
   B. prepare the performance appraisal reports on your staff members
   C. represent your unit in dealings with the heads of other units
   D. handle matters that require exception to general policy

4. In establishing rules for his subordinates, a superior should be PRIMARILY concerned with
   A. creating sufficient flexibility to allow for exceptions
   B. making employees aware of the reasons for the rules and the penalties for infractions
   C. establishing the strength of his own position in relation to his subordinates
   D. having his subordinates know that such rules will be imposed in a personal manner

5. The practice of conducting staff training sessions on a periodic basis is *generally* considered
   A. *poor*; it takes employees away from their work assignments
   B. *poor*; all staff training should be done on an individual basis
   C. *good*; it permits the regular introduction of new methods and techniques
   D. *good*; it ensures a high employee productivity rate

6. Suppose you have just announced at a staff meeting with your subordinates that a radical reorganization of work will take place next week. Your subordinates at the meeting appear to be excited, tense, and worried.
   Of the following, the BEST action for you to take at that time is to
   A. schedule private conferences with each subordinate to obtain his reaction to the meeting
   B. close the meeting and tell your subordinates to return immediately to their work assignments
   C. give your subordinates some time to ask questions and discuss your announcement
   D. insist that your subordinates do not discuss your announcement among themselves or with other members of the agency

7. Assume that you supervise the duplicating and reproduction unit of Department B. One of your responsibilities is to prepare a daily schedule showing when and on which of your unit's four duplicating machines jobs are to be run off.
   Of the following, the factor that should be given LEAST consideration in preparing the schedule is the
   A. priority of each of the jobs to be run off
   B. production speed of the different machines that will be used
   C. staff available to operate the machines
   D. date on which the job order was received

8. Suppose that you were recently placed in charge of the 8. ...
duplicating and stock unit of Department Y. From your
observation of the operations of your unit during your
first week as its head, you get the impression that there
are inefficiencies in its operations causing low productivity.
To obtain an increase in its productivity, the FIRST of the
following actions you should take is to
  A. seek the advice of your immediate superior on how he
     would tackle this problem
  B. develop plans to correct any unsatisfactory conditions
     arising from other than manpower deficiencies
  C. identify the problems causing low productivity
  D. discuss your productivity problem with other unit heads
     to find out how they handled similar problems

9. Assume that you were recently placed in charge of a large 9. ...
clerical unit. At a meeting, the head of another unit
tells you, "My practice is to give a worker more than he
can finish. In that way you can be sure that you are getting
the most out of him."
For you to adopt this practice would be
  A. *advisable*, since your actions would be consistent with
     those practiced in your agency
  B. *inadvisable*, since such a practice is apt to create
     frustration and lower staff morale
  C. *advisable*, since a high goal stimulates people to
     strive to attain it
  D. *inadvisable*, since management may, in turn, set too
     high a productivity goal for the unit

10. Suppose that you are the supervisor of a unit in which 10. ...
there is an increasing amount of friction among several
of your staff members. One of the reasons for this friction is that the work of some of these staff members cannot
be completed by them until other staff members complete related work.
Of the following, the MOST appropriate action for you to
take is to
  A. summon these employees to a meeting to discuss the
     responsibilities each has and to devise better
     methods of coordination
  B. have a private talk with each employee involved and
     make each understand that there must be more coopera-
     tion among the employees
  C. arrange for interviews with each of the employees
     involved to determine what his problems are
  D. shift the assignments of these employees so that each
     will be doing a job different from his current one

11. An office supervisor has a number of responsibilities with 11. ...
regard to his subordinates.
Which one of the following functions should NOT be regarded
as a *basic* responsibility of the office supervisor?
  A. Telling employees how to solve personal problems that
     may be interfering with their work
  B. Training new employees to do the work assigned to them
  C. Evaluating employees' performance periodically and
     discussing the evaluation with each employee

D. Bringing employee grievances to the attention of higher-level administrators and seeking satisfactory resolutions

12. One of your most productive subordinates frequently demonstrates a poor attitude toward his job. He seems unsure of himself, and he annoys his co-workers because he is continually belittling himself and the work that he is doing.
In trying to help him overcome this problem, which of the following approaches is LEAST likely to be effective?

   12. ...

   A. Compliment him on his work and assign him some additional responsibilities, telling him that he is being given these responsibilities because of his demonstrated ability

   B. Discuss with him the problem of his attitude, and warn him that you will have to report it on his next performance evaluation

   C. Assign him a particularly important and difficult project, stressing your confidence in his ability to complete it successfully

   D. Discuss with him the problem of his attitude, and ask him for suggestions as to how you can help him overcome it

13. You come to realize that a personality conflict between you and one of your subordinates is adversely affecting his performance.
Which one of the following would be the most appropriate FIRST step to take?

   13. ...

   A. Report the problem to your superior and request assistance. His experience may be helpful in resolving this problem

   B. Discuss the situation with several of the subordinate's co-workers to see if they can suggest any remedy

   C. Suggest to the subordinate that he get professional counseling or therapy

   D. Discuss the situation candidly with the subordinate, with the objective of resolving the problem between yourselves

KEY (CORRECT ANSWERS)

TEST 1				TEST 2				TEST 3			
1.	C	11.	D	1.	C	11.	A	1.	C	7.	D
2.	B	12.	A	2.	C	12.	A	2.	D	8.	C
3.	A	13.	A	3.	C	13.	A	3.	A	9.	B
4.	C	14.	B	4.	C	14.	C	4.	B	10.	A
5.	C	15.	D	5.	B	15.	B	5.	C	11.	A
6.	A	16.	C	6.	D	16.	B	6.	C	12.	B
7.	C	17.	D	7.	D	17.	D			13.	D
8.	C	18.	D	8.	D	18.	A				
9.	C	19.	D	9.	A	19.	D				
10.	D	20.	C	10.	A	20.	A				
		21.	B			21.	C				
		22.	C			22.	B				
		23.	C			23.	D				
		24.	B			24.	B				
		25.	D			25.	C				

EXAMINATION SECTION
TEST 1

DIRECTIONS: Each question or incomplete statement is followed by several suggested answers or completions. Select the one that BEST answers the question or completes the statement. *PRINT THE LETTER OF THE CORRECT ANSWER IN THE SPACE AT THE RIGHT.*

1. Professional staff members in large organizations are sometimes frustrated by a lack of vital work-related information because of the failure of some middle-management supervisors to pass along unrestricted information from top management.
All of the following are considered to be reasons for such failure to pass along information EXCEPT the supervisors'

    A. belief that information affecting procedures will be ignored unless they are present to supervise their subordinates
    B. fear that specific information will require explanation or justification
    C. inclination to regard the possession of information as a symbol of higher status
    D. tendency to treat information as private property

1.____

2. Increasingly in government, employees' records are being handled by automated data processing systems. However, employees frequently doubt a computer's ability to handle their records properly.
Which of the following is the BEST way for management to overcome such doubts?

    A. Conduct a public relations campaign to explain the savings certain to result from the use of computers
    B. Use automated data processing equipment made by the firm which has the best repair facilities in the industry
    C. Maintain a clerical force to spot check on the accuracy of the computer's record-keeping
    D. Establish automated data processing systems that are objective, impartial, and take into account individual factors as far as possible

2.____

3. Some management experts question the usefulness of offering cash to individual employees for their suggestions.
Which of the following reasons for opposing cash awards is MOST valid?

    A. Emphasis on individual gain deters cooperative effort.
    B. Money spent on evaluating suggestions may outweigh the value of the suggestions.
    C. Awards encourage employees to think about unusual methods of doing work.
    D. Suggestions too technical for ordinary evaluation are usually presented.

3.____

4. The use of outside consultants, rather than regular staff, in studying and recommending improvements in the operations of public agencies has been criticized.
Of the following, the BEST argument in favor of using regular staff is that such staff can better perform the work because they

    A. are more knowledgeable about operations and problems
    B. can more easily be organized into teams consisting of technical specialists
    C. may wish to gain additional professional experience
    D. will provide reports which will be more interesting to the public since they are more experienced

4.____

5. One approach to organizational problem-solving is to have all problem-solving authority   5.__
   centralized at the top of the organization.
   However, from the viewpoint of providing maximum service to the public, this practice
   is UNWISE chiefly because it

    A. reduces the responsibility of the decision-makers
    B. produces delays
    C. reduces internal communications
    D. requires specialists

6. Research has shown that problem-solving efficiency is optimal when the motivation of   6.__
   the problem-solver is at a moderate rather than an extreme level.
   Of the following, probably the CHIEF reason for this is that the problem-solver

    A. will cause confusion among his subordinates when his motivation is too high
    B. must avoid alternate solutions that tend to lead him up blind alleys
    C. can devote his attention to both the immediate problem as well as to other relevant
       problems in the general area
    D. must feel the need to solve the problem but not so urgently as to direct all his atten-
       tion to the need and none to the means of solution

7. Don't be afraid to make mistakes. Many organizations are paralyzed from the fear of   7.__
   making mistakes. As a result, they don't do the things they should; they don't try new and
   different ideas.
   For the effective supervisor, the MOST valid implication of this statement is that

    A. mistakes should not be encouraged, but there are some unavoidable risks in deci-
       sion-making
    B. mistakes which stem from trying new and different ideas are usually not serious
    C. the possibility of doing things wrong is limited by one's organizational position
    D. the fear of making mistakes will prevent future errors

8. The duties of an employee under your supervision may be either routine, problem-solv-   8.__
   ing, innovative, or creative. Which of the following BEST describes duties which are both
   innovative and creative?

    A. Checking to make sure that work is done properly
    B. Applying principles in a practical manner
    C. Developing new and better methods of meeting goals
    D. Working at two or more jobs at the same time

9. According to modern management theory, a supervisor who uses as little authority as   9.__
   possible and as much as is necessary would be considered to be using a mode that is

    A. autocratic   B. inappropriate
    C. participative   D. directive

10. Delegation involves establishing and maintaining effective working arrangements   10._____
between a supervisor and the persons who report to him.
Delegation is MOST likely to have taken place when the

   A. entire staff openly discusses common problems in order to reach solutions satis-
      factory to the supervisor
   B. performance of specified work is entrusted to a capable person, and the expected
      results are mutually understood
   C. persons assigned to properly accomplish work are carefully evaluated and given a
      chance to explain shortcomings
   D. supervisor provides specific written instructions in order to prevent anxiety on the
      part of inexperienced persons

11. Supervisors often are not aware of the effect that their behavior has on their subordi-   11._____
nates.
The one of the following training methods which would be BEST for changing such
supervisory behavior is

   A. essential skills training
   B. off-the-job training
   C. sensitivity training
   D. developmental training

12. A supervisor, in his role as a trainer, may have to decide on the length and frequency of   12._____
training sessions.
When the material to be taught is new, difficult, and lengthy, the trainer should be
guided by the principle that for BEST results in such circumstances, sessions should
be

   A. longer, relatively fewer in number, and held on successive days
   B. shorter, relatively greater in number, and spaced at intervals of several days
   C. of average length, relatively fewer in number, and held at intermittent intervals
   D. of random length and frequency, but spaced at fixed intervals

13. Employee training which is based on realistic simulation, sometimes known as *game*   13._____
play or *role play*, is sometimes preferable to learning from actual experience on the
job. Which of the following is NOT a correct statement concerning the value of simulation
to trainees?

   A. Simulation allows for practice in decision-making without any need for subsequent
      discussion.
   B. Simulation is intrinsically motivating because it offers a variety of challenges.
   C. Compared to other, more traditional training techniques, simulation is dynamic.
   D. The simulation environment is nonpunitive as compared to real life.

14. Programmed instruction as a method of training has all of the following advantages   14._____
EXCEPT:

   A. Learning is accomplished in an optimum sequence of distinct steps
   B. Trainees have wide latitude in deciding what is to be learned within each program
   C. The trainee takes an active part in the learning process
   D. The trainee receives immediate knowledge of the results of his response

15. In a work-study program, trainees were required to submit weekly written performance reports in order to insure that work assignments fulfilled the program objectives. Such reports would also assist the administrator of the work-study program PRIMA-RILY to

    A. eliminate personal counseling for the trainees
    B. identify problems requiring prompt resolution
    C. reduce the amount of clerical work for all concerned
    D. estimate the rate at which budgeted funds are being expended

    15.___

16. Which of the following would be MOST useful in order to avoid misunderstanding when preparing correspondence or reports?

    A. Use vocabulary which is at an elementary level
    B. Present each sentence as an individual paragraph
    C. Have someone other than the writer read the material for clarity
    D. Use general words which are open to interpretation

    16.___

17. Which of the following supervisory methods would be MOST likely to train subordinates to give a prompt response to memoranda in an organizational setting where most trans-actions are informal?

    A. Issue a written directive setting forth a schedule of strict deadlines
    B. Let it be known, informally, that those who respond promptly will be rewarded
    C. Follow up each memorandum by a personal inquiry regarding the receiver's reaction to it
    D. Direct subordinates to furnish a precise explanation for ignoring memos

    17.___

18. Conferences may fail for a number of reasons. Still, a conference that is an apparent fail-ure may have some benefit.
Which of the following would LEAST likely be such a benefit? It may

    A. increase for most participants their possessiveness about information they have
    B. produce a climate of good will and trust among many of the participants
    C. provide most participants with an opportunity to learn things about the others
    D. serve as a unifying force to keep most of the individuals functioning as a group

    18.___

19. Assume that you have been assigned to study and suggest improvements in an operat-ing unit of a delegate agency whose staff has become overwhelmed with problems, has had inadequate resources, and has become accustomed to things getting worse. The staff is indifferent to cooperating with you because they see no hope of improvement. Which of the following steps would be LEAST useful in carrying out your assignment?

    A. Encourage the entire staff to make suggestions to you for change
    B. Inform the staff that management is somewhat dissatisfied with their performance
    C. Let staff know that you are fully aware of their problems and stresses
    D. Look for those problem areas where changes can be made quickly

    19.___

20. Which of the following statements about employer-employee relations is NOT consid-   20._____
ered to be correct by leading managerial experts?

    A.   An important factor in good employer-employee relations is treating workers
respectfully.
    B.   Employer-employee relations are profoundly influenced by the fundamentals of
human nature.
    C.   Good employer-employee relations must stem from top management and reach
downward.
    D.   Employee unions are usually a major obstacle to establishing good employer-
employee relations.

21. In connection with labor relations, the term *management rights* GENERALLY refers to   21._____

    A.   a managerial review level in a grievance system
    B.   statutory prohibitions that bar monetary negotiations
    C.   the impact of collective bargaining on government
    D.   those subjects which management considers to be non-negotiable

22. Barriers may exist to the utilization of women in higher level positions. Some of these   22._____
barriers are attitudinal in nature.
Which of the following is MOST clearly attitudinal in nature?

    A.   Advancement opportunities which are vertical in nature and thus require seniority
    B.   Experience which is inadequate or irrelevant to the needs of a dynamic and pro-
gressive organization
    C.   Inadequate means of early identification of employees with talent and potential for
advancement
    D.   Lack of self-confidence on the part of some women concerning their ability to han-
dle a higher position

23. Because a reader reacts to the meaning he associates with a word, we can never be   23._____
sure what emotional impact a word may carry or how it may affect our readers.
The MOST logical implication of this statement for employees who correspond with
members of the public is that

    A.   a writer should try to select a neutral word that will not bias his writing by its hidden
emotional meaning
    B.   simple language should be used in writing letters denying requests so that readers
are not upset by the denial
    C.   every writer should adopt a writing style which he finds natural and easy
    D.   whenever there is any doubt as to how a word is defined, the dictionary should be
consulted

24. A public information program should be based on clear information about the nature of   24._____
actual public knowledge and opinion. One way of learning about the views of the public is
through the use of questionnaires.
Which of the following is of LEAST importance in designing a questionnaire?

    A.   A respondent should be asked for his name and address.
    B.   A respondent should be asked to choose from among several statements the one
which expresses his views.
    C.   Questions should ask for responses in a form suitable for processing.
    D.   Questions should be stated in familiar language.

25. Assume that you have accepted an invitation to speak before an interested group about 25.___
a problem. You have brought with you for distribution a number of booklets and other
informational material.
Of the following, which would be the BEST way to use this material?

    A. Distribute it before you begin talking so that the audience may read it at their lei-
sure.
    B. Distribute it during your talk to increase the likelihood that it will be read.
    C. Hold it until the end of your talk, then announce that those who wish may take or
examine the material.
    D. Before starting the talk, leave it on a table in the back of the room so that people
may pick it up as they enter.

KEY (CORRECT ANSWERS)

1.	A		11.	C
2.	D		12.	B
3.	A		13.	A
4.	A		14.	B
5.	B		15.	B
6.	D		16.	C
7.	A		17.	C
8.	C		18.	A
9.	C		19.	B
10.	B		20.	D

21.	D
22.	D
23.	A
24.	A
25.	C

TEST 2

DIRECTIONS: Each question or incomplete statement is followed by several suggested answers or completions. Select the one that BEST answers the question or completes the statement. *PRINT THE LETTER OF THE CORRECT ANSWER IN THE SPACE AT THE RIGHT.*

1. Of the following, the FIRST step in planning an operation is to   1.____

    A. obtain relevant information
    B. identify the goal to be achieved
    C. consider possible alternatives
    D. make necessary assignments

2. A supervisor who is extremely busy performing routine tasks is MOST likely making   2.____
INCORRECT use of what basic principle of supervision?

    A. Homogeneous Assignment   B. Span of Control
    C. Work Distribution   D. Delegation of Authority

3. Controls help supervisors to obtain information from which they can determine whether   3.____
their staffs are achieving planned goals.
Which one of the following would be LEAST useful as a control device?

    A. Employee diaries   B. Organization charts
    C. Periodic inspections   D. Progress charts

4. A certain employee has difficulty in effectively performing a particular portion of his rou-   4.____
tine assignments, but his overall productivity is average.
As the direct supervisor of this individual, your BEST course of action would be to

    A. attempt to develop the man's capacity to execute the problematical facets of his assignments
    B. diversify the employee's work assignments in order to build up his confidence
    C. reassign the man to less difficult tasks
    D. request in a private conversation that the employee improve his work output

5. A supervisor who uses persuasion as a means of supervising a unit would GENERALLY   5.____
also use which of the following practices to supervise his unit?

    A. Supervise and control the staff with an authoritative attitude to indicate that he is a *take-charge* individual
    B. Make significant changes in the organizational operations so as to improve job efficiency
    C. Remove major communication barriers between himself, subordinates, and management
    D. Supervise everyday operations while being mindful of the problems of his subordinates

6. Whenever a supervisor in charge of a unit delegates a routine task to a capable subordi-   6.____
nate, he tells him exactly how to do it.
This practice is GENERALLY

    A. *desirable,* chiefly because good supervisors should be aware of the traits of their subordinates and delegate responsibilities to them accordingly
    B. *undesirable,* chiefly because only non–routine tasks should be delegated
    C. *desirable,* chiefly because a supervisor should frequently test the willingness of his subordinates to perform ordinary tasks
    D. *undesirable,* chiefly because a capable subordinate should usually be allowed to exercise his own discretion in doing a routine job

7. The one of the following activities through which a supervisor BEST demonstrates leadership ability is by   7

    A. arranging periodic staff meetings in order to keep his subordinates informed about professional developments in the field

    B. frequently issuing definite orders and directives which will lessen the need for subordinates to make decisions in handling any tasks assigned to them

    C. devoting the major part of his time to supervising subordinates so as to stimulate continuous improvement

    D. setting aside time for self-development and research so as to improve the skills, techniques, and procedures of his unit

8. The following three statements relate to the supervision of employees: 8.__

    I. The assignment of difficult tasks that offer a challenge is more conducive to good morale than the assignment of easy tasks

    II. The same general principles of supervision that apply to men are equally applicable to women

    III. The best retraining program should cover all phases of an employee's work in a general manner

Which of the following choices list ALL of the above statements that are generally correct?

    A. II, III   B. I
    C. I, II   D. I, II, III

9. Which of the following examples BEST illustrates the application of the *exception principle* as a supervisory technique?   9

    A. A complex job is divided among several employees who work simultaneously to complete the whole job in a shorter time.

    B. An employee is required to complete any task delegated to him to such an extent that nothing is left for the superior who delegated the task except to approve it.

    C. A superior delegates responsibility to a subordinate but retains authority to make the final decisions.

    D. A superior delegates all work possible to his subordinates and retains that which requires his personal attention or performance.

10. Assume that you are a supervisor. Your immediate superior frequently gives orders to your subordinates without your knowledge.   10.__
Of the following, the MOST direct and effective way for you to handle this problem is to

    A. tell your subordinates to take orders only from you

    B. submit a report to higher authority in which you cite specific instances

    C. discuss it with your immediate superior

    D. find out to what extent your authority and prestige as a supervisor have been affected

11. In an agency which has as its primary purpose the protection of the public against fraudulent business practices, which of the following would GENERALLY be considered an *auxiliary* or *staff* rather than a *line* function?   11.__

    A. Interviewing victims of frauds and advising them about their legal remedies

    B. Daily activities directed toward prevention of fraudulent business practices

    C. Keeping records and statistics about business violations reported and corrected

    D. Follow-up inspections by investigators after corrective action has been taken

12. A supervisor can MOST effectively reduce the spread of false rumors through the *grapevine* by   12.____

    A. identifying and disciplining any subordinate responsible for initiating such rumors
    B. keeping his subordinates informed as much as possible about matters affecting them
    C. denying false rumors which might tend to lower staff morale and productivity
    D. making sure confidential matters are kept secure from access by unauthorized employees

13. A supervisor has tried to learn about the background, education, and family relationships of his subordinates through observation, personal contact, and inspection of their personnel records.   13.____
These supervisory actions are GENERALLY

    A. *inadvisable,* chiefly because they may lead to charges of favoritism
    B. *advisable,* chiefly because they may make him more popular with his subordinates
    C. *inadvisable,* chiefly because his efforts may be regarded as an invasion of privacy
    D. *advisable,* chiefly because the information may enable him to develop better understanding of each of his subordinates

14. In an emergency situation, when action must be taken immediately, it is BEST for the supervisor to give orders in the form of   14.____

    A. direct commands which are brief and precise
    B. requests, so that his subordinates will not become alarmed
    C. suggestions which offer alternative courses of action
    D. implied directives, so that his subordinates may use their judgment in carrying them out

15. When demonstrating a new and complex procedure to a group of subordinates, it is ESSENTIAL that a supervisor   15.____

    A. go slowly and repeat the steps involved at least once
    B. show the employees common errors and the consequences of such errors
    C. go through the process at the usual speed so that the employees can see the rate at which they should work
    D. distribute summaries of the procedure during the demonstration and instruct his subordinates to refer to them afterwards

16. After a procedures manual has been written and distributed,   16.____

    A. continuous maintenance work is necessary to keep the manual current
    B. it is best to issue new manuals rather than make changes in the original manual
    C. no changes should be necessary
    D. only major changes should be considered

17. Of the following, the MOST important criterion of effective report writing is

    A. eloquence of writing style
    B. the use of technical language
    C. to be brief and to the point
    D. to cover all details

17._

18. The use of electronic data processing

    A. has proven unsuccessful in most organizations
    B. has unquestionable advantages for all organizations
    C. is unnecessary in most organizations
    D. should be decided upon only after careful feasibility studies by individual organizations

18._

19. The PRIMARY purpose of work measurement is to

    A. design and install a wage incentive program
    B. determine who should be promoted
    C. establish a yardstick to determine extent of progress
    D. set up a spirit of competition among employees

19._

20. The action which is MOST effective in gaining acceptance of a study by the agency which is being studied is

    A. a directive from the agency head to install a study based on recommendations included in a report
    B. a lecture-type presentation following approval of the procedures
    C. a written procedure in narrative form covering the proposed system with visual presentations and discussions
    D. procedural charts showing the *before* situation, forms, steps, etc., to the employees affected

20._

21. Which organization principle is MOST closely related to procedural analysis and improvement?

    A. Duplication, overlapping, and conflict should be eliminated.
    B. Managerial authority should be clearly defined.
    C. The objectives of the organization should be clearly defined.
    D. Top management should be freed of burdensome detail.

21._

22. Which one of the following is the MAJOR objective of operational audits?

    A. Detecting fraud
    B. Determining organization problems
    C. Determining the number of personnel needed
    D. Recommending opportunities for improving operating and management practices

22._

23. Of the following, the formalization of organization structure is BEST achieved by

    A. a narrative description of the plan of organization
    B. functional charts
    C. job descriptions together with organization charts
    D. multi-flow charts

23._

24. Budget planning is MOST useful when it achieves 24.____

    A. cost control   B. forecast of receipts
    C. performance review   D. personnel reduction

25. GENERALLY, in applying the principle of delegation in dealing with subordinates, a 25.____
supervisor

    A. allows his subordinates to set up work goals and to fix the limits within which they
can work
    B. allows his subordinates to set up work goals and then gives detailed orders as to
how they are to be achieved
    C. makes relatively few decisions by himself and frames his orders in broad, general
terms
    D. provides externalized motivation for his subordinates

KEY (CORRECT ANSWERS)

1.	B		11.	C
2.	D		12.	B
3.	B		13.	D
4.	A		14.	A
5.	D		15.	A
6.	D		16.	A
7.	C		17.	C
8.	C		18.	D
9.	D		19.	C
10.	C		20.	C

21.	A
22.	D
23.	C
24.	A
25.	C

EXAMINATION SECTION
TEST 1

DIRECTIONS: Each question or incomplete statement is followed by several suggested answers or completions. Select the one that BEST answers the question or completes the statement. *PRINT THE LETTER OF THE CORRECT ANSWER IN THE SPACE AT THE RIGHT.*

1. At times there may be a conflict between employees' needs and agency goals. A supervisor's MAIN role in motivating employees in such circumstances is to try to   1._____

   A. develop good work habits among the employees whom he supervises
   B. emphasize the importance of material rewards such as merit increases
   C. keep careful records of employees' performance for possible disciplinary action
   D. reconcile employees' objectives with those of the public agency

2. Organizations cannot function effectively without policies. However, when an organization imposes excessively detailed policy restrictions, it is MOST likely to lead to   2._____

   A. conflicts among individual employees
   B. a lack of adequate supervision
   C. a reduction of employee initiative
   D. a reliance on punitive discipline

3. The PRIMARY responsibility for establishing good employee relations in the public service USUALLY rests with   3._____

   A. employees   B. management
   C. civil service organizations   D. employee organizations

4. At times, certain off-the-job conduct of public employees may be of concern to management. This concern stems from the fact that   4._____

   A. agency programs could be harmed by adverse publicity if employees' conduct is considered detrimental by the public
   B. fairness to all concerned is usually the major consideration in disciplinary cases
   C. public employees must meet higher standards than employees working in private industry
   D. public employees have high ethical standards and may participate in social action programs

5. At one time or another, most employees ask for, or expect, special treatment. For a supervisor faced with this problem, the one of the following which is the MOST valid guideline is: 5._____

   A. According to the rules, a supervisor must give identical treatment to all his subordinates, regardless of the circumstances.
   B. Although all employees have equal rights, it is sometimes necessary to give an employee special treatment to meet an individual need.
   C. It would damage morale if any employee were to receive special treatment, regardless of circumstances.
   D. Since each employee has different needs, there is little reason to maintain general rules.

6. Mental health problems exist in many parts of our society and may also be found in the work setting. The BASIC role of the supervisor in relation to the mental health problems of his subordinates is to

    A.   restrict himself solely to the taking of disciplinary measures, if warranted, and follow up carefully
    B.   avoid involvement in personal matters
    C.   identify mental health problems as early as possible
    D.   resolve mental health problems through personal counseling

7. Supervisory expectation of high levels of employee performance, where such performance is possible, is MOST likely to lead to employees'

    A.   expecting frequent praise and encouragement
    B.   gaining a greater sense of satisfaction
    C.   needing less detailed instructions then previously
    D.   reducing their quantitative output

8. In public agencies, as elsewhere, supervisors sometimes compete with one another to increase their units' productivity. Of the following, the MAJOR disadvantage of such competition, from the general viewpoint of providing good public service, is that

    A.   while individual employee effort will increase, unit productivity will decrease
    B.   employees will be discouraged from sincere interest in their work
    C.   the supervisors' competition may hinder the achievement of agency goals
    D.   total payroll costs will increase as the activities of each unit increase

9. If employees are motivated primarily by material compensation, the amount of effort an individual employee will put into performing his work effectively will depend MAINLY upon how he perceives

    A.   cooperation to be tied to successful effort
    B.   the association between good work and increased compensation
    C.   the public status of his particular position
    D.   the supervisor's behavior in work situations

10. Cash awards to individual employees are sometimes used to encourage useful suggestions. However, some management experts believe that awards should involve some form of employee recognition other than cash. Which of the following reasons BEST supports opposition to using cash as a reward for worthwhile suggestions?

    A.   Cash awards cause employees to expend excessive time in making suggestions.
    B.   Taxpayer opposition to cash awards has increased following generous salary increases for public employees in recent years.
    C.   Public funds expended on awards lead to a poor image of public employees.
    D.   The use of cash awards raises the problem of deciding tne monetary value of suggestions.

11. The BEST general rule for a supervisor to follow in giving praise and criticism is to

    A.   criticize and praise publicly
    B.   criticize publicly and praise privately
    C.   praise and criticize privately
    D.   praise publicly and criticize privately

12. An important step in designing an error-control policy is to determine the maximum num-　12._____
ber of errors that can be considered acceptable for the entire organization. Of the following, the MOST important factor in making such a decision is the

    A. number of clerical staff available to check for errors
    B. frequency of errors by supervisors
    C. human and material costs of errors
    D. number of errors that will become known to the public

13. When a supervisor tries to correct a situation where errors have been widespread, he　13._____
should concentrate his efforts, and those of the employees involved, on

    A. avoiding future mistakes   B. fixing appropriate blame
    C. preparing a written report   D. determining fair penalties

14. When delegating work to a subordinate, a supervisor should ALWAYS tell the subordi-　14._____
nate

    A. each step in the procedure for doing the work
    B. how much time to expend
    C. what is to be accomplished
    D. whether reports are necessary

15. The responsibilities of all employees should be clearly defined and understood. In addi-　15._____
tion, in order for employees to successfully fulfill their responsibilities, they should also
GENERALLY be given

    A. written directives   B. close supervision
    C. corresponding authority   D. daily instructions

16. The one of the following types of training in which positive transfer of training to the　16._____
actual work situation is MOST likely to take place is

    A. conference training   B. demonstration training
    C. classroom training   D. on-the-job training

17. The type of training or instruction in which the subject matter is presented in small units　17._____
called frames is known as

    A. programmed instruction   B. reinforcement
    C. remediation   D. skills training

18. In order to bring about maximum learning in a training situation, a supervisor acting as a　18._____
trainer should attempt to create a setting in which

    A. all trainees experience a large amount of failure as an incentive
    B. all trainees experience a small amount of failure as an incentive
    C. each trainee experiences approximately the same amounts of success and failure
    D. each trainee experiences as much success and as little failure as possible

19. Assume that, in a training course given by an agency, the instructor conducts a brief quiz, on paper, toward the close of each session. From the point of view of maximizing learning, it would be BEST for the instructor to

    A. wait until the last session to provide the correct answers
    B. give the correct answers aloud immediately after each quiz
    C. permit trainees to take the questions home with them so that they can look up the answers
    D. wait until the next session to provide the correct answers

19.___

20. A supervisor, in the course of evaluating employees, should ALWAYS determine whether

    A. employees realize that their work is under scrutiny
    B. the ratings will be included in permanent records
    C. employees meet standards of performance
    D. his statements on the rating form are similar to those made by the previous supervisor

20.___

21. All of the following are legitimate objectives of employee performance reporting systems EXCEPT

    A. serving as a check on personnel policies such as job qualification requirements and placement techniques
    B. determining who is the least efficient worker among a large number of employees
    C. improving employee performance by identifying strong and weak points in individual performance
    D. developing standards of satisfactory performance

21.___

22. Studies of existing employee performance evaluation schemes have revealed a common tendency to construct guides in order to measure inferred traits. Of the following, the BEST example of an inferred trait is

    A. appearance   B. loyalty   C. accuracy   D. promptness

22.___

23. Which of the following is MOST likely to be a positive influence in promoting common agreement at a staff conference?

    A. A mature, tolerant group of participants
    B. A strong chairman with firm opinions
    C. The normal differences of human personalities
    D. The urge to forcefully support one's views

23.___

24. Before holding a problem-solving conference, the conference leader sent to each invitee an announcement on which he listed the names of all invitees. His action in listing the names was

    A. *wise,* mainly because all invitees will know who has been invited, and can, if necessary, plan a proper approach
    B. *unwise,* mainly because certain invitees could form factions prior to the conference
    C. *unwise,* mainly because invitees might come to the conference in a belligerent mood if they had had interpersonal conflicts with other invitees
    D. *wise,* mainly because invitees who are antagonistic to each other could decide not to attend

24.___

25. Methods analysis is a detailed study of existing or proposed work methods for the purpose of improving agency operations. Of the following, it is MOST accurate to say that
this type of study

    A. can sometimes be made informally by the experienced supervisor who can identify
       problems and suggest solutions
    B. is not suitable for studying the operations of a public agency
    C. will be successfully accomplished only if an outside organization reviews agency
       operations
    D. usually costs more to complete than is justified by the potential economies to be
       realized

25.____

———

KEY (CORRECT ANSWERS)

1.	D		11.	D
2.	C		12.	C
3.	B		13.	A
4.	A		14.	C
5.	B		15.	C
6.	C		16.	D
7.	B		17.	A
8.	C		18.	D
9.	B		19.	B
10.	D		20.	C

21.	B
22.	B
23.	A
24.	A
25.	A

———

TEST 2

DIRECTIONS: Each question or incomplete statement is followed by several suggested answers or completions. Select the one that BEST answers the question or completes the statement. *PRINT THE LETTER OF THE CORRECT ANSWER IN THE SPACE AT THE RIGHT.*

1. Present-day managerial practices advocate that adequate hierarchical levels of communication be maintained among all levels of management. Of the following, the BEST way to accomplish this is with   1._

    A. interdepartmental memoranda only
    B. interdepartmental memoranda only
    C. periodic staff meetings, interdepartmental and interdepartmental memoranda
    D. interdepartmental and interdepartmental memoranda

2. It is generally agreed upon that it is important to have effective communications in the unit so that everyone knows exactly what is expected of him. Of the following, the communications system which can assist in fulfilling this objective BEST is one which consists of   2._

    A. written policies and procedures for administrative functions and verbal policies and procedures for professional functions
    B. written policies and procedures for professional and administrative functions
    C. verbal policies and procedures for professional and administrative functions
    D. verbal policies and procedures for professional functions

3. If a department manager wishes to build an effective department, he MOST generally must   3.

    A. be able to hire and fire as he feels necessary
    B. consider the total aspects of his job, his influence and the effects of his decisions
    C. have access to reasonable amounts of personnel and money with which to build his programs
    D. attend as many professional conferences as possible so that he can keep up-to-date with all the latest advances in the field

4. Of the following, the factor which generally contributes MOST effectively to the performance of the unit is that the supervisor   4._

    A. personally inspect the work of all employees
    B. fill orders at a faster rate than his subordinates
    C. have an exact knowledge of theory
    D. implement a program of professional development for his staff

5. Administrative policies relate MOST closely to   5._

    A. control of commodities and personnel
    B. general policies emanating from the central office
    C. fiscal management of the department only
    D. handling and dispensing of funds

6. Part of being a good supervisor is to be able to develop an attitude towards employees which will motivate them to do their best on the job. The GOOD supervisor, therefore, should

    A. take an interest in subordinates, but not develop an all-consuming attitude in this area
    B. remain in an aloof position when dealing with employees
    C. be as close to subordinates as possible on the job
    D. take a complete interest in all the activities of subordinates, both on and off the job

6.____

7. The practice of a supervisor assigning an experienced employee to train new employees instead of training them himself, is, GENERALLY, considered

    A. *undesirable*; the more experienced employee will resent being taken away from his regular job
    B. *desirable*; the supervisor can then devote more time to his regular duties
    C. *undesirable*; the more experienced employee is not working at the proper level to train new employees
    D. *desirable*; the more experienced employee is probably a better trainer than the supervisor

7.____

8. It is generally agreed that on-the-job training is MOST effective when new employees are

    A. provided with study manuals, standard operating procedures and other written materials to be studied for at least two weeks before the employees attempt to do the job
    B. shown how to do the job in detail, and then instructed to do the work under close supervision
    C. trained by an experienced worker for at least a week to make certain that the employees can do the job
    D. given work immediately which is checked at the end of each day

8.____

9. Employees sometimes form small informal groups, commonly called cliques. With regard to the effect of such groups on processing of the workload, the attitude a supervisor should take towards these cliques is that of

    A. *acceptance*, since they take the employees' minds off their work without wasting too much time
    B. *rejection*, since those workers inside the clique tend to do less work than the out-siders
    C. *acceptance*, since the supervisor is usually included in the clique
    D. *rejection*, since they are usually disliked by higher management

9.____

10. Of the following, the BEST statement regarding rules and regulations in a unit is that they

    A. are "necessary evils" to be tolerated by those at and above the first supervisory level only
    B. are stated in broad, indefinite terms so as to allow maximum amount of leeway in complying with them
    C. must be understood by all employees in the unit
    D. are primarily for management's needs since insurance regulations mandate them

10.____

11. It is sometimes considered desirable for a supervisor to survey the opinions of his employees before taking action on decisions affecting them. Of the following, the greatest DISADVANTAGE of following this approach is that the employees might

    A. use this opportunity to complain rather than to make constructive suggestions
    B. lose respect for their supervisor whom they feel cannot make his own decisions
    C. regard this as an attempt by the supervisor to get ideas for which he can later claim credit
    D. be resentful if their suggestions are not adopted

12. Of the following, the MOST important reason for keeping statements of duties of employees up-to-date is to

    A. serve as a basis of information for other governmental jurisdictions
    B. enable the department of personnel to develop job-related examinations
    C. differentiate between levels within the occupational groups
    D. enable each employee to know what his duties are

13. Of the following, the BEST way to evaluate the progress of a new subordinate is to

    A. compare the output of the new employee from week to week as to quantity and quality
    B. obtain the opinions of the new employee's co-workers
    C. test the new employee periodically to see how much he has learned
    D. hold frequent discussions with the employee focusing on his work

14. Of the following, a supervisor is LEAST likely to contribute to good morale in the unit if he

    A. encourages employees to increase their knowledge and proficiency in their work on their own time
    B. reprimands subordinates uniformly when infractions are committed
    C. refuses to accept explanations for mistakes regardless of who has made them or how serious they are
    D. compliments subordinates for superior work performance in the presence of their peers

15. The practice of promoting supervisors from within a given unit only, rather than from within the entire agency, may BEST be described as

    A. *desirable*, because the type of work in each unit generally is substantially different from all other units
    B. *undesirable*, since it will severely reduce the number of eligibles from which to select a supervisor
    C. *desirable*, since it enables each employee to know in advance the precise extent of promotion opportunities in his unit
    D. *undesirable*, because it creates numerous administrative and budgetary difficulties

16. Of the following, the BEST way for a supervisor to make assignments GENERALLY is to

    A. give the easier assignments to employees with greater seniority
    B. give the difficult assignments to the employees with greater seniority
    C. make assignments according to the ability of each employee
    D. rotate the assignments among the employees

17. Assume that a supervisor makes a proposal through appropriate channels which would delegate final authority and responsibility to a subordinate employee for a major control function within the agency. According to current management theory, this proposal should be

    A. *adopted,* since this would enable the supervisor to devote more time to non-routine tasks

    B. *rejected,* since final responsibility for this high-level assignment may not properly be delegated to a subordinate employee

    C. *adopted,* since the assignment of increased responsibility to subordinate employees is a vital part of their development and training

    D. *rejected,* since the morale of the subordinate employees not selected for this assignment would be adversely affected

17.____

18. If it becomes necessary for a supervisor to improve the performance of a subordinate to assure the achievement of results according to plans, the BEST course of action, of the following, generally, would be to

    A. emphasize the subordinate's strengths and try to motivate the employee to improve on those factors

    B. emphasize the subordinate's weak areas of performance and try to bring them up to an acceptable standard

    C. issue a memorandum to all employees warning that if performance does not improve, disciplinary measures will be taken

    D. transfer the subordinate to another section engaged in different work

18.____

19. A supervisor who specifies each phase of a job in detail, supervises closely and permits very little discretion in performance of tasks, GENERALLY

    A. provides motivation for his staff to produce more work

    B. finds that his subordinates make fewer mistakes than those with minimal supervision

    C. finds that his subordinates have little or no incentive to work any harder than necessary

    D. provides superior training opportunities for his employees

19.____

20. Assume that you supervise two employees who do not get along well with each other. Their relationship has been continuously deteriorating. You decide to take steps to solve this problem by first determining the reason for their inability to get along well with each other. This course of action is

    A. *desirable,* because their work is probably adversely affected by their differences

    B. *undesirable,* because your inquiries might be is-interpreted by the employees and cause resentment

    C. *desirable,* because you could then learn who is at fault for causing the deteriorating relationship and take appropriate disciplinary measures

    D. *undesirable,* because it is best to let them work their differences out between themselves

20.____

21. Routine procedures that have worked well in the past should be reviewed periodically by a supervisor MAINLY because

    A. they may have become outdated or in need of revision
    B. employees may dislike the procedures even though they have proven successful in the past
    C. these reviews are the main part of a supervisor's job
    D. this practice serves to give the supervisor an idea of how productive his subordinates are

22. Assume that an employee tells his supervisor about a grievance he has against a co-worker. The supervisor assures the employee that he will immediately take action to eliminate the grievance. The supervisor's attitude should be considered

    A. *correct*; because a good supervisor is one who can come to a quick decision
    B. *incorrect*; because the supervisor should have told the employee that he will investigate the grievance and then determine a future course of action
    C. *correct*; because the employee's morale will be higher, resulting in greater productivity
    D. *incorrect*; because the supervisor should remain uninvolved and let the employees settle grievances between themselves

23. If an employee's work output is low and of poor quality due to faulty work habits, the MOST constructive of the following ways for a supervisor to correct this situation, GENERALLY, is to

    A. discipline the employee
    B. transfer the employee to another unit
    C. provide additional training
    D. check the employee's work continuously

24. Assume that it becomes necessary for a supervisor to ask his staff to work overtime. Which one of the following techniques is MOST likely to win their willing cooperation to do this?

    A. Point out that this is part of their job specification entitled "performs related work"
    B. Explain the reason it is necessary for the employees to work overtime
    C. Promise the employees special consideration regarding future leave matters
    D. Warn that if the employees do not work overtime, they will face possible disciplinary action

25. If an employee's work performance has recently fallen below established minimum standards for quality and quantity, the threat of demotion or other disciplinary measures as an attempt to improve this employee's performance would probably be the MOST acceptable and effective course of action

    A. *only* after other more constructive measures have failed
    B. *if* applied uniformly to all employees as soon as performance falls below standard
    C. *only* if the employee understands that the threat will not actually be carried out
    D. *if* the employee is promised that, as soon as his work performance improves, he will be reinstated to his previous status

KEY (CORRECT ANSWERS)

1.	C		11.	D
2.	B		12.	D
3.	B		13.	A
4.	D		14.	C
5.	A		15.	B
6.	A		16.	C
7.	B		17.	B
8.	B		18.	B
9.	A		19.	C
10.	C		20.	A

21.	A
22.	B
23.	C
24.	B
25.	A

TEST 3

DIRECTIONS: Each question or incomplete statement is followed by several suggested answers or completions. Select the one that BEST answers the question or completes the statement. *PRINT THE LETTER OF THE CORRECT ANSWER IN THE SPACE AT THE RIGHT.*

1. If, as a supervisor, it becomes necessary for you to assign an employee to supervise your unit during your vacation, it would generally be BEST to select the employee who

    A.   is the best technician on the staff
    B.   can get the work out smoothly, without friction
    C.   has the most seniority
    D.   is the most popular with the group

1.___

2. Assume that, as a supervisor, your own work has accumulated to the point where you decide that it is desirable for you to delegate in order to meet your deadlines. The one of the following tasks which would be MOST appropriate to delegate to a subordinate is

    A.   checking the work of the employees for accuracy
    B.   attending a staff conference at which implementation of a new departmental policy will be discussed
    C.   preparing a final report including a recommendation on purchase of expensive new laboratory equipment
    D.   preparing final budget estimates for next year's budget

2.___

3. Of the following actions, the one LEAST appropriate for you to take during an *initial* interview with a new employee is to

    A.   find out about the experience and education of the new employee
    B.   attempt to determine for what job in your unit the employee would best be suited
    C.   tell the employee about his duties and responsibilities
    D.   ascertain whether the employee will make good promotion material

3.___

4. If it becomes necessary to reprimand a subordinate employee, the BEST of the following ways to do this is to

    A.   ask the employee to stay after working hours and then reprimand him
    B.   reprimand the employee immediately after the infraction has been committed
    C.   take the employee aside and speak to him privately during regular working hours
    D.   write a short memo to the employee warning that strict adherence to departmental policy and procedures is required of all employees

4.___

5. If you, as a supervisor, believe that one of your subordinate employees has a serious problem, such as alcoholism or an emotional disturbance, which is adversely affecting his work, the BEST way to handle this situation *initially* would be to

    A.   urge him to seek proper professional help before he is dismissed from his job
    B.   ignore it and let the employee work out the problem himself
    C.   suggest that the employee take an extended leave of absence until he can again function effectively
    D.   frankly tell the employee that unless his work improves, you will take disciplinary measures against him

5.___

6. Of the following, the BEST way to develop a subordinate's potential is to   6.____

    A. give him a fair chance to learn by doing
    B. assign him more than his share of work
    C. criticize only his work
    D. urge him to do his work rapidly

7. During a survey, an employee from another agency asks you to assist him on a job which   7.____
would require a full day of your time. Of the following, the BEST immediate action for you
to take is to

    A. refuse to assist him
    B. ask for compensation before doing it
    C. assist him promptly
    D. notify his department head

8. Of the following, the BEST way to handle an overly talkative subordinate is to   8.____

    A. have your superior talk to him about it
    B. have a subordinate talk to him about it
    C. talk to him about it in a group conference
    D. talk to him about it in private

9. While you are making a survey, a citizen questions you about the work you are doing. Of   9.____
the following, the BEST thing to do is to

    A. answer the questions tactfully
    B. refuse to answer any questions
    C. advise him to write a letter to the main office
    D. answer the questions in double-talk

10. Respect for a supervisor is MOST likely to increase if he is   10.____

    A. morose   B. sporadic   C. vindictive   D. zealous

11. A subordinate who continuously bypasses his immediate supervisor for technical infor-   11.____
mation should be

    A. reprimanded by his immediate supervisor
    B. ignored by his immediate supervisor
    C. given more difficult work to do
    D. given less difficult work to do

12. Complicated instructions should NOT be written   12.____

    A. accurately   B. lucidly   C. factually   D. verbosely

13. Of the following, the MOST important reason for checking a report is to   13.____

    A. check accuracy   B. eliminate unnecessary sections
    C. catch mistakes   D. check for delineation

14. Two subordinates under your supervision dislike each other to the extent that production 14
is cut down. Your BEST action as a supervisor is to

    A. ignore the matter and hope for the best
    B. transfer the more aggressive man
    C. cut down on the work load
    D. talk to them together about the matter

15. One of the following characteristics which a supervisor should NOT display while explain- 15.__
ing a job to a subordinate is

    A. enthusiasm   B. confidence
    C. apathy   D. determination

16. Of the following, for BEST production of work, it should be assigned according to a per- 16.__
son's

    A. attitude toward the work   B. ability to do the work
    C. salary   D. seniority

17. You receive an anonymous written complaint from a citizen about a subordinate who 17.__
used abusive language. Of the following, your BEST course of action is to

    A. ignore the letter
    B. report it to your supervisor
    C. discuss the complaint with the subordinate privately
    D. keep the subordinate in the office

18. A supervisor should recognize that the way to get the BEST results from his instructions 18.__
and assignments to the staff is to use

    A. a suggestive approach after he has decided exactly what is to be done and how
    B. the willing and cooperative staff members and avoid the hard-to-handle people
    C. care to select the persons most capable of carrying out the assignments
    D. an authoritative, non-nonsense tone when issuing instructions or giving assign-
       ments

19. As the supervisor of a unit, you find that you are spending too much of your time on rou- 19.__
tine tasks and not enough on coordinating the work of the staff or preparing necessary
reports. Of the following, it would be MOST advisable for you to

    A. discard a great portion of the routine jobs done in the unit
    B. give some of the routine jobs to other members of the staff
    C. postpone the routine jobs and concentrate on coordinating the work of the staff
    D. delegate the job of coordinating the work to the most capable member of the staff

20. At times a supervisor may be called upon to train new employees. Suppose that you are 20.__
giving such training in several sessions to be held on different days. During the first session, a trainee interrupts everal times to ask questions at key points in your discussion.
Of the following, the BEST way to handle this trainee is to

    A. advise him to pay closer attention so he can avoid asking too many questions
    B. tell him to listen without interrupting and he'll hear his questions answered

    C.   answer his questions to show him that you know your field, but make a mental note that this trainee is a troublemaker

    D.   answer each question fully and make certain he understands the answers

21.   Employee errors can be reduced to a minimum by effective supervision and by training. Which of the following approaches used by a supervisor would usually be MOST effective in handling an employee who has made an avoidable and serious error for the first time?   21._____

    A.   Tell the worker how other employees avoid making errors

    B.   Analyze with the employee the situation leading to the error and then take whatever administrative or training steps are needed to avoid such errors

    C.   Use this error as the basis for a staff meeting at which the employee's error is disclosed and discussed in an effort to improve the performance

    D.   Urge the employee to modify his behavior in light of his mistake

22.   Suppose that a particular staff member, formerly one of your most regular workers, has recently fallen into the habit of arriving a bit late to work several times a week. You feel that such a habit can grow consistently worse and spread to other staff members unless it is checked. Of the following, the BEST action for you to take, as the supervisor in charge of the unit, is to   22._____

    A.   go immediately to your own supervisor, present the facts, and have this employee disciplined

    B.   speak privately to this tardy employee, advise him of the need to improve his punctuality, and inform him that he'll be disciplined if late again

    C.   talk to the co-worker with whom this late employee is most friendly and ask the friend to help him solve his tardiness problem

    D.   speak privately with this employee, and try to discover and deal with the reasons for the latenesses

23.   A supervisor may make an assignment in the form of a request, a command, or a call for volunteers. It is LEAST desirable to make an assignment in the form of a request when   23._____

    A.   an employee does not like the particular kind of assignment to be given

    B.   the assignment requires working past the regular closing day

    C.   an emergency has come up

    D.   the assignment is not particularly pleasant for anybody

24.   When you give a certain task that you normally perform yourself to one of your employees, it is MOST important that you   24._____

    A.   lead the employee to believe that he has been chosen above others to perform this job

    B.   describe the job as important even though it is merely a routine task

    C.   explain the job that needs to be accomplished, but always let the employee decide how to do it

    D.   tell the employee why you are delegating the job to him and explain exactly what he is to do

25. A supervisor when instructing new trainees in the routine of his unit should include a
description of the department's overall objectives and programs in order to

    A. insure that individual work assignments will be completed satisfactorily
    B. create a favorable impression of his supervisory capabilities
    C. develop a better understanding of the purposes behind work assignments
    D. produce an immediate feeling of group cooperation

_____

KEY (CORRECT ANSWERS)

1.	B		11.	A	
2.	A		12.	D	
3.	D		13.	C	
4.	C		14.	D	
5.	A		15.	C	
6.	A		16.	B	
7.	A		17.	C	
8.	D		18.	C	
9.	A		19.	B	
10.	D		20.	D	

21.	B
22.	D
23.	A
24.	D
25.	C

_____

TEST 4

DIRECTIONS: Each question or incomplete statement is followed by several suggested answers or completions. Select the one that BEST answers the question or completes the statement. *PRINT THE LETTER OF THE CORRECT ANSWER IN THE SPACE AT THE RIGHT.*

1. An integral part of every supervisor's job is getting his ideas or instructions across to his staff. The extent of his success, if he has a reasonably competent staff, is PRIMARILY dependent on the

    A. interest of the employee
    B. intelligence of the employee
    C. reasoning behind the ideas or instructions
    D. presentation of the ideas or instructions

1.____

2. Generally, what is the FIRST action the supervisor should take when an employee approaches him with a complaint?

    A. Review the employee's recent performance with him
    B. Use the complaint as a basis to discuss improvement of procedures
    C. Find out from the employee the details of the complaint
    D. Advise the employee to take his complaint to the head of the department

2.____

3. Of the following, which is NOT usually considered one of the purposes of counseling an employee after an evaluation of his performance?

    A. Explaining the performance standards used by the supervisor
    B. Discussing necessary disciplinary action to be taken
    C. Emphasizing the employee's strengths and weaknesses
    D. Planning better utilization of the employee's strengths

3.____

4. Assume that a supervisor, when reviewing a decision reached by one of his subordinates, finds the decision incorrect. Under these circumstances, it would be MOST desirable for the supervisor to

    A. correct the decision and inform the subordinate of this at a staff meeting
    B. correct the decision and suggest a more detailed analysis in the future
    C. help the employee find the reason for the correct decision
    D. refrain from assigning this type of a problem to the employee

4.____

5. An IMPORTANT characteristic of a good supervisor is his ability to

    A. be a stern disciplinarian
    B. put off the settling of grievances
    C. solve problems   D. find fault in individuals

5.____

6. A new supervisor will BEST obtain the respect of the men assigned to him if he

    A. makes decisions rapidly and sticks to them, regardless of whether they are right or wrong
    B. makes decisions rapidly and then changes them just as rapidly if the decisions are wrong
    C. does not make any decisions unless he is absolutely sure that they are right
    D. makes his decisions after considering carefully all available information

6.____

7. A newly appointed worker is operating at a level of performance below that of the other employees. In this situation, a supervisor should FIRST

    A. lower the acceptable standard for the new man
    B. find out why the new man cannot do as well as the others
    C. advise the new worker he will be dropped from the payroll at the end of the probationary period
    D. assign another new worker to assist the first man

8. Assume that you have to instruct a new man on a specific departmental operation. The new man seems unsure of what you have said. Of the following, the BEST way for you to determine whether the man has understood you is to

    A. have the man explain the operation to you in his own words
    B. repeat your explanation to him slowly
    C. repeat your explanation to him, using simpler wording
    D. emphasize the important parts of the operation to him

9. A supervisor realizes that he has taken an instanteous dislike to a new worker assigned to him. The BEST course of action for the supervisor to take in this case is to

    A. be especially observant of the new worker's actions
    B. request that the new worker be reassigned
    C. make a special effort to be fair to the new worker
    D. ask to be transferred himself

10. A supervisor gives detailed instructions to his men as to how a certain type of job is to be done. One ADVANTAGE of this practice is that this will

    A. result in a more flexible operation
    B. standardize operations
    C. encourage new men to learn
    D. encourage initiative in the men

11. Of the following, the one that would MOST likely be the result of poor planning is:

    A. Omissions are discovered after the work is completed.
    B. During the course of normal inspection, a meter is found to be inaccessible.
    C. An inspector completes his assignments for that day ahead of schedule.
    D. A problem arises during an inspection and prevents an inspector from completing his day's assignments.

12. Of the following, the BEST way for a supervisor to maintain good employee morale is for the supervisor to

    A. avoid correcting the employee when he makes mistakes
    B. continually praise the employee's work even when it is of average quality
    C. show that he is willing to assist in solving the employee's problems
    D. accept the employee's excuses for failure even though the excuses are not valid

13. A supervisor takes time to explain to his men why a departmental order has been issued.   13._____
This practice is

     A. *good,* mainly because without this explanation the men will not be able to carry out the order
     B. *bad,* mainly because time will be wasted for no useful purpose
     C. *good,* because understanding the reasons behind an order will lead to more effective carrying out of the order
     D. *bad,* because men will then question every order that they receive

14. Of the following, the MOST important responsibility of a supervisor in charge of a section   14._____
is to

     A. establish close personal relationships with each of his subordinates in the section
     B. insure that each subordinate in the section knows the full range of his duties and responsibilities
     C. maintain friendly relations with his immediate supervisor
     D. protect his subordinates from criticism from any source

15. The BEST way to get a good work output from employees is to   15._____

     A. hold over them the threat of disciplinary action or removal
     B. maintain a steady, unrelenting pressure on them
     C. show them that you can do anything they can do faster and better
     D. win their respect and liking, so they want to work for you

---

KEY (CORRECT ANSWERS)

1.	A		6.	D
2.	C		7.	B
3.	A		8.	A
4.	C		9.	C
5.	C		10.	B

11.	A
12.	C
13.	C
14.	B
15.	D

WORD SUBSTITUTION
EXAMINATION SECTION
TEST 1

DIRECTIONS: Each question or incomplete statement is followed by several suggested answers or completions. Select the one that BEST answers the question or completes the statement. *PRINT THE LETTER OF THE CORRECT ANSWER IN THE SPACE AT THE RIGHT.*

Questions 1-5.

DIRECTIONS: Each of Questions 1 through 5 consists of a statement which contains one word that is INCORRECTLY used because it is not in keeping with the meaning that the statement is evidently intended to convey. Determine which word is incorrectly used. Select from the choices lettered A, B, C, and D the word which, when substituted for the incorrectly used word, would BEST help to convey the meaning of the statement.

1. A complex society like our own, after all, depends on the skills of the individuals compos-   1____
    ing it. Concerns of human safety, convenience, and the quality of our collective life are of
    as great consequence as our concern for equal protection of the laws. We do want a
    qualified surgeon when we need an operation. We assume a skilled pilot, especially
    when it is we who are on the plane. We want the telephone to work, and our mail to come
    to us, and not to someone down the street. We want competent teachers for our children.
    In universities, we want high standards of scholarship and research.
    Our existence places us at the mercy of persons, never invisible to us, who are certi-
    fied for their qualities. While we may argue about the manner in which, in real life, skill
    and competence are elicited and ascertained, we can hardly argue that there are no
    such things as skill and competence or that there is no way of measuring them. But
    there are those among us who do make this argument and those who also accept it,
    and its spreading influence may well constitute the single greatest threat to the quality
    of our lives today.

    A. little   B. quibble
    C. gullibility   D. often

2. If strategy or policy does not further plans or make enterprise procedures more attain-   2____
    able, it has not done its job. No manager should ever be able to say: There's no good
    reason why we do it, it is just our policy! While many policies and some strategies are, in
    effect, permanent, it should never be assumed that they represent natural laws engraved
    on stone. If goals, premises, or major plans change, strategies and policies should be
    reconsidered to meet the new situation.

    A. objectives   B. exclaim
    C. diverge   D. reinforced

3. To some extent, the attitude that experience is the best teacher is justifiable. The very   3
    fact that the manager has reached his position appears to justify his decisions. Moreover,
    the reasoning process of thinking problems through, making decisions, and seeing pro-
    grams succeed or fail, does make for a degree of good judgment (at times bordering on
    the intuitive). Many people, however, do not profit by their errors, and there are managers
    who seen never to gain the seasoned judgment required by modern enterprise.
    There is danger, however, in relying on one's past experience as a guide for future
    action. In the first place, it is an unusual human being who recognizes the obvious rea-
    sons for his mistakes or failures. In the second place, the lessons of experience may
    be entirely unsuitable to new problems. Good decisions must be evaluated against
    future events, while experience belongs to the past.

    A. poorest   B. underlying
    C. principle   D. quantified

4. A bit of thinking will give a clue to the variety of disciplines which are involved in the   4___
    range of the personnel function. In staffing - from initial entry to promotion and transfer
    the field of psychological measurement is brought into play. Compensation decisions
    require economists and statisticians. Job analysis calls for skills in research and adminis-
    trative procedure. Training draws upon adult education specialists and other occupa-
    tions. Health and safety measures demand the employment of medical doctors, nurses,
    and safety engineers. Operating a retirement system necessitates expertise in the insur-
    ance field and actuarial mathematics. Dealing with employees corporately requires
    knowledge in labor relations. Interpretation of rules and adjudication of claims and com-
    plaints call for the skills of lawyers. And all the elements of leadership, budgeting, incen-
    tive, evaluation, and discipline, on which the personnel program is expected to provide
    the principal guidance, can be fortified only by a liberal understanding of such social sci-
    ences as social psychology and sociology, to say nothing of a healthy dose of that con-
    ventional wisdom known as common sense.

    A. supervision   B. physiological
    C. economic   D. purchasing

5. Another means of increasing participation is what has been called *grass roots* budgeting.   5___
    Instead of a budget for operations or capital expenditures being prepared at the top or
    departmental level, the smallest organization units prepare their budgets and submit
    them upward. Naturally, to be effective, these units must be aware of objectives, policies,
    and programs which affect their operations, must above all be given clear planning preri-
    ises, and be furnished factors enabling them to convert work load into requirements for
    men, material, and money. If these budget requests are reviewed and coordinated by
    departmental management, and if the budget makers are required to expend their bud-
    gets, this means of planning participation becomes real and purposeful. There probably
    exist no greater incentive to planning and no stronger sense of participation than those
    created in developing, defending, and selling a course of action over which the manager
    has control and for which he bears responsibility.

    A. intermediate   B. productivity
    C. defend   D. cut

KEY (CORRECT ANSWERS)

1. D
2. A
3. B
4. A
5. C

———

TEST 2

DIRECTIONS: Each question or incomplete statement is followed by several suggested answers or completions. Select the one that BEST answers the question or completes the statement. *PRINT THE LETTER OF THE CORRECT ANSWER IN THE SPACE AT THE RIGHT.*

Questions 1-5.

DIRECTIONS: Each of Questions 1 through 5 consists of a paragraph which contains one word that is incorrectly used because it is not in keeping with the meaning that the paragraph is evidently intended to convey. This word will be found in that portion of the paragraph which is underlined. Read the entire paragraph. Then determine which word is incorrectly used. Select from the choices lettered A, B, C, and D the word which, when substituted for the incorrectly used word, would BEST help to convey the meaning of the quotation.

1. In plotting its manpower course, an organization has to make assumptions about   1__
    changes ahead in the next 5, 10, 15, or 20 years. The most profound changes will occur
    in people themselves, particularly in young people. The fact is that today's young people
    are much better educated than their counterparts of 20 and 30 years ago, are much
    more likely to react negatively to blind authority and to have different ideas about trans-
    portation to work. While the transformation may not show up as readily in young busi-
    ness managers, they must be taken into account because they most certainly will have a
    profound effect upon management style and management potential in the next 20 years.

    A. contemporary   B. evolve
    C. favorably   D. motivation

2. The need for flexibility has an important bearing on the time span that programs should   2__
    cover. The very existence of a program inhibits some loss of flexibility. By reason of hav-
    ing adopted it, the agency reduces its freedom, to do something different in future years,
    since a conscious act of revision is required. On the other hand investment projects, to
    say nothing of research and development, undertaken now must be based on some view
    of a highly uncertain future. Time spans should be long enough but not unnecessarily
    long. The dilemma could be partially resolved if programs could be expressed in terms of
    ranges rather than single figures. If the ranges included genuine upper and lower limits, it
    would become clear that projection beyond a limited period was not operationally mean-
    ingful.

    A. counteracts   B. lag
    C. accelerated   D. implies

3. The tendency to delude ourselves into believing that organizations largely run themselves is why there are so many counterfeits in the management ranks. Such persons
are glib, intelligent, persuasive, personable, and even charming. But once on the executive staff they will produce little and destroy more. Sometimes a counterfeit manager can
get by for years in a company by the simple device of not remaining in the same job for
more than two years. Long-range effects usually are felt first in the intervening variables
such as employee loyalties, attitudes, and motivations. These variables affect the end-
result variables such as productivity and earnings much more slowly, so that the outcome
is difficult to trace back to a specific manager. Managerial effectiveness becomes, therefore, an explicit quality, greatly to be desired but difficult to pinpoint. Advances in the
behavioral sciences are making inroads. We now know that only certain types of personalities have the talent to achieve excellence in management positions.

3____

    A. concomitant   B. elusive
    C. encroachments   D. simulated

4. The implementation of appropriation decisions without distortion or deceit is an important
element in the maintenance of democratic institutions. The people must control the public purse through the judgments of their elected representatives and the performance of
their civil servants. This is the foundation of public confidence and trust. However, honest
and faithful execution of appropriation decisions is not enough. What about the preparation of those decisions whose undeviating performance has been guaranteed? Is a
democracy effectively administered if it does not clearly identify its objectives and its
resources and rationally allocate scarce means to ensure achievement of these objectives? A budget appropriately designed to meet the requirements of a rational decision-
making process will not, of course, automatically ensure the making of rational decisions.
But it can be a powerful influence in that direction.

4____

    A. approval   B. recognize
    C. adherence   D. quality

5. How effective is a program in attaining its intended objective? Can existing program
results be accomplished at lower cost? These questions attempt to draw a distinction
between the *effectiveness* of a program in achieving its objective and the *efficiency* with
which it is carried out. For instance, if it is possible to consider the effectiveness of the
rent control program under the present organization of the office, it should also be possible to decide whether the same results could be more efficiently achieved by reorganization. Efficiency might be increased by having fewer senior attorneys and more assistants,
or vice versa. The distinction between effectiveness and efficiency must, however, be
used with extreme care. Measures that purport to increase efficiency generally have a
negligible effect, good or bad, on effectiveness. Government economy campaigns, for
instance, often greatly reduce effectiveness in the guise of merely increasing office efficiency.

5____

    A. augment   B. pronounced
    C. purposefully   D. improving

KEY (CORRECT ANSWERS)

1. D
2. D
3. B
4. D
5. B

———

READING COMPREHENSION
UNDERSTANDING AND INTERPRETING WRITTEN MATERIAL
EXAMINATION SECTION
TEST 1

DIRECTIONS: Each question or incomplete statement is followed by several suggested answers or completions. Select the one that BEST answers the question or completes the statement. *PRINT THE LETTER OF THE CORRECT ANSWER IN THE SPACE AT THE RIGHT.*

Questions 1-5.

DIRECTIONS: Questions 1 through 5 are to be answered SOLELY on the basis of the following passage.

The most effective control mechanism to prevent gross incompetence on the part of public employees is a good personnel program. The personnel officer in the line departments and the central personnel agency should exert positive leadership to raise levels of performance. Although the key factor is the quality of the personnel recruited, staff members other than personnel officers can make important contributions to efficiency. Administrative analysts, now employed in many agencies, make detailed studies of organization and procedures, with the purpose of eliminating delays, waste, and other inefficiencies. Efficiency is, however, more than a question of good organization and procedures; it is also the product of the attitudes and values of the public employees. Personal motivation can provide the will to be efficient. The best management studies will not result in substantial improvement of the performance of those employees who feel no great urge to work up to their abilities.

1. The above passage indicates that the KEY factor in preventing gross incompetence of public employees is the

    A. hiring of administrative analysts to assist personnel people
    B. utilization of effective management studies
    C. overlapping of responsibility
    D. quality of the employees hired

    1.____

2. According to the above passage, the central personnel agency staff SHOULD

    A. work more closely with administrative analysts in the line departments than with personnel officers
    B. make a serious effort to avoid jurisdictional conflicts with personnel officers in line departments
    C. contribute to improving the quality of work of public employees
    D. engage in a comprehensive program to change the public's negative image of public employees

    2.____

3. The above passage indicates that efficiency in an organization can BEST be brought about by

    A. eliminating ineffective control mechanisms
    B. instituting sound organizational procedures

    3.____

    C.   promoting competent personnel
    D.   recruiting people with desire to do good work

4.   According to the above passage, the purpose of administrative analysis in a public   4.__
     agency is to

    A.   prevent injustice to the public employee
    B.   promote the efficiency of the agency
    C.   protect the interests of the public
    D.   ensure the observance of procedural due process

5.   The above passage implies that a considerable rise in the quality of work of public   5.__
     employees can be brought about by

    A.   encouraging positive employee attitudes toward work
    B.   controlling personnel officers who exceed their powers
    C.   creating warm personal associations among public employees in an agency
    D.   closing loopholes in personnel organization and procedures

Questions 6-8.

DIRECTIONS: Questions 6 through 8 are to be answered SOLELY on the basis of the follow-
                ing passage on Employee Needs.

EMPLOYEE NEEDS

The greatest waste in industry and in government may be that of human resources. This waste usually derives not from employees' unwillingness or inability, but from management's ineptness to meet the maintenance and motivational needs of employees. Maintenance needs refer to such needs as providing employees with safe places to work, written work rules, job security, adequate salary, employer-sponsored social activities, and with knowledge of their role in the overall framework of the organization. However, of greatest significance to employees are the motivational needs of job growth, achievement, responsibility, and recognition.

Although employee dissatisfaction may stem from either poor maintenance or poor motivation factors, the outward manifestation of the dissatisfaction may be very much alike, i.e., negativism, complaints, deterioration of performance, and so forth. The improvement in the lighting of an employee's work area or raising his level of pay won't do much good if the source of the dissatisfaction is the absence of a meaningful assignment. By the same token, if an employee is dissatisfied with what he considers inequitable pay, the introduction of additional challenge in his work may simply make matters worse.

It is relatively easy for an employee to express frustration by complaining about pay, washroom conditions, fringe benefits, and so forth; but most people cannot easily express resentment in terms of the more abstract concepts concerning job growth, responsibility, and achievement.

It would be wrong to assume that there is no interaction between maintenance and motivational needs of employees. For example, conditions of high motivation often overshadow poor maintenance conditions. If an organization is in a period of strong growth and expansion, opportunities for job growth, responsibility, recognition, and achievement are usually abundant, but the rapid growth may have outrun the upkeep of maintenance factors. In this situation, motivation may be high, but only if employees recognize the poor maintenance conditions as unavoidable and temporary. The subordination of maintenance factors cannot go on indefinitely, even with the highest motivation.

Both maintenance and motivation factors influence the behavior of all employees, but employees are not identical and, furthermore, the needs of any individual do not remain constant. However, a broad distinction can be made between employees who have a basic orientation toward maintenance factors and those with greater sensitivity toward motivation factors.

A highly maintenance-oriented individual, preoccupied with the factors peripheral to his job rather than the job itself, is more concerned with comfort than challenge. He does not get deeply involved with his work but does with the condition of his work area, toilet facilities, and his time for going to lunch. By contrast, a strongly motivation-oriented employee is usually relatively indifferent to his surroundings and is caught up in the pursuit of work goals.

Fortunately, there are few people who are either exclusively maintenance-oriented or purely motivation-oriented. The former would be deadwood in an organization, while the latter might trample on those around him in his pursuit to achieve his goals.

6. With respect to employee motivational and maintenance needs, the management policies of an organization which is growing rapidly will probably result   6._____

    A.   more in meeting motivational needs rather than maintenance needs
    B.   more in meeting maintenance needs rather than motivational needs
    C.   in meeting both of these needs equally
    D.   in increased effort to define the motivational and maintenance needs of its employees

7. In accordance with the above passage, which of the following CANNOT be considered as an example of an employee maintenance need for railroad clerks?   7._____

    A.   Providing more relief periods
    B.   Providing fair salary increases at periodic intervals
    C.   Increasing job responsibilities
    D.   Increasing health insurance benefits

8. Most employees in an organization may be categorized as being interested in   8._____

    A.   maintenance needs *only*
    B.   motivational needs *only*
    C.   both motivational and maintenance needs
    D.   money only, to the exclusion of all other needs

Questions 9-11.

DIRECTIONS: Questions 9 through 11 are to be answered SOLELY on the basis of the following passage on Good Employee Practices.

GOOD EMPLOYEE PRACTICES

As a city employee, you will be expected to take an interest in your work and perform the duties of your job to the best of your ability and in a spirit of cooperation. Nothing shows an interest in your work more than coming to work on time, not only at the start of the day but also when returning from lunch. If it is necessary for you to keep a personal appointment at lunch hour which might cause a delay in getting back to work on time, you should explain the situation to your supervisor and get his approval to come back a little late before you leave for lunch.

You should do everything that is asked of you willingly and consider important even the small jobs that your supervisor gives you. Although these jobs may seem unimportant, if you forget to do them or if you don't do them right, trouble may develop later.

Getting along well with your fellow workers will add much to the enjoyment of your work. You should respect your fellow workers and try to see their side when a disagreement arises. The better you get along with your fellow workers and your supervisor, the better you will like your job and the better you will be able to do it.

9. According to the above passage, in your job as a city employee, you are expected to   9.__

    A. show a willingness to cooperate on the job
    B. get your supervisor's approval before keeping any personal appointments at lunch hour
    C. avoid doing small jobs that seem unimportant
    D. do the easier jobs at the start of the day and the more difficult ones later on

10. According to the above passage, getting to work on time shows that you   10.__

    A. need the job
    B. have an interest in your work
    C. get along well with your fellow workers
    D. like your supervisor

11. According to the above passage, the one of the following statements that is NOT true is   11.__

    A. if you do a small job wrong, trouble may develop
    B. you should respect your fellow workers
    C. if you disagree with a fellow worker, you should try to see his side of the story
    D. the less you get along with your supervisor, the better you will be able to do your job

Questions 12-15.

DIRECTIONS: Questions 12 through 15 are to be answered SOLELY on the basis of the following passage on Employee Suggestions.

EMPLOYEE SUGGESTIONS

To increase the effectiveness of the city government, the city asks its employees to offer suggestions when they feel an improvement could be made in some government operation. The Employees' Suggestions Program was started to encourage city employees to do this.

Through this Program, which is only for city employees, cash awards may be given to those whose suggestions are submitted and approved. Suggestions are looked for not only from supervisors but from all city employees as any city employee may get an idea which might be approved and contribute greatly to the solution of some problem of city government

Therefore, all suggestions for improvement are welcome, whether they be suggestions on how to improve working conditions, or on how to increase the speed with which work is done, or on how to reduce or eliminate such things as waste, time losses, accidents or fire hazards. There are, however, a few types of suggestions for which cash awards cannot be given. An example of this type would be a suggestion to increase salaries or a suggestion to change the regulations about annual leave or about sick leave. The number of suggestions sent in has increased sharply during the past few years. It is hoped that it will keep increasing in the future in order to meet the city's needs for more ideas for improved ways of doing things.

12. According to the above passage, the MAIN reason why the city asks its employees for suggestions about government operations is to   12._____

    A.   increase the effectiveness of the city government
    B.   show that the Employees' Suggestion Program is working well
    C.   show that everybody helps run the city government
    D.   have the employee win a prize

13. According to the above passage, the Employees' Suggestion Program can approve awards ONLY for those suggestions that come from   13._____

    A.   city employees
    B.   city employees who are supervisors
    C.   city employees who are not supervisors
    D.   experienced employees of the city

14. According to the above passage, a cash award cannot be given through the Employees' Suggestion Program for a suggestion about   14._____

    A.   getting work done faster
    B.   helping prevent accidents on the job
    C.   increasing the amount of annual leave for city employees
    D.   reducing the chance of fire where city employees work

15. According to the above passage, the suggestions sent in during the past few years have   15._____

    A.   all been approved
    B.   generally been well written
    C.   been mostly about reducing or eliminating waste
    D.   been greater in number than before

Questions 16-18.

DIRECTIONS: Questions 16 through 18 are to be answered SOLELY on the basis of the following passage.

The supervisor will gain the respect of the members of his staff and increase his influence over them by controlling his temper and avoiding criticizing anyone publicly. When a mistake is made, the good supervisor will talk it over with the employee quietly and privately. The supervisor will listen to the employee's story, suggest the better way of doing the job, and offer help so the mistake won't happen again. Before closing the discussion, the supervisor should try to find something good to say about other parts of the employee's work. Some praise and appreciation, along with instruction, is more likely to encourage an employee to improve in those areas where he is weakest.

16. A good title that would show the meaning of the above passage would be

    A. HOW TO CORRECT EMPLOYEE ERRORS
    B. HOW TO PRAISE EMPLOYEES
    C. MISTAKES ARE PREVENTABLE
    D. THE WEAK EMPLOYEE

16.__

17. According to the above passage, the work of an employee who has made a mistake is more likely to improve if the supervisor

    A. avoids criticizing him
    B. gives him a chance to suggest a better way of doing the work
    C. listens to the employee's excuses to see if he is right
    D. praises good work at the same time he corrects the mistake

17.__

18. According to the above passage, when a supervisor needs to correct an employee's mistake, it is important that he

    A. allow some time to go by after the mistake is made
    B. do so when other employees are not present
    C. show his influence with his tone of voice
    D. tell other employees to avoid the same mistake

18.__

Questions 19-23.

DIRECTIONS: Questions 19 through 23 are to be answered SOLELY on the basis of the following passage.

In studying the relationships of people to the organizational structure, it is absolutely necessary to identify and recognize the informal organizational structure. These relationships are necessary when coordination of a plan is attempted. They may be with *the boss,* line supervisors, staff personnel, or other representatives of the formal organization's hierarchy, and they may include the *liaison men* who serve as the leaders of the informal organization. An acquaintanceship with the people serving in these roles in the organization, and its formal counterpart, permits a supervisor to recognize sensitive areas in which it is simple to get a conflict reaction. Avoidance of such areas, plus conscious efforts to inform other people of his own objectives for various plans, will usually enlist their aid and support. Planning *without people* can lead to disaster because the individuals who must act together to make any plan a success are more important than the plans themselves.

19. Of the following titles, the one that MOST clearly describes the above passage is

    A. COORDINATION OF A FUNCTION
    B. AVOIDANCE OF CONFLICT
    C. PLANNING WITH PEOPLE
    D. PLANNING OBJECTIVES

19.__

20. According to the above passage, attempts at coordinating plans may fail unless   20.____

    A. the plan's objectives are clearly set forth
    B. conflict between groups is resolved
    C. the plans themselves are worthwhile
    D. informal relationships are recognized

21. According to the above passage, conflict   21.____

    A. may, in some cases, be desirable to secure results
    B. produces more heat than light
    C. should be avoided at all costs
    D. possibilities can be predicted by a sensitive supervisor

22. The above passage implies that   22.____

    A. informal relationships are more important than formal structure
    B. the weakness of a formal structure depends upon informal relationships
    C. liaison men are the key people to consult when taking formal and informal structures into account
    D. individuals in a group are at least as important as the plans for the group

23. The above passage suggests that   23.____

    A. some planning can be disastrous
    B. certain people in sensitive areas should be avoided
    C. the supervisor should discourage acquaintanceships in the organization
    D. organizational relationships should be consciously limited

Questions 24-25.

DIRECTIONS: Questions 24 and 25 are to be answered SOLELY on the basis of the following passage.

Good personnel relations of an organization depend upon mutual confidence, trust, and good will. The basis of confidence is understanding. Most troubles start with people who do not understand each other. When the organization's intentions or motives are misunderstood, or when reasons for actions, practices, or policies are misconstrued, complete cooperation from individuals is not forthcoming. If management expects full cooperation from employees, it has a responsibility of sharing with them the information which is the foundation of proper understanding, confidence, and trust. Personnel management has long since outgrown the days when it was the vogue to *treat them rough and tell them nothing.* Up-to-date personnel management provides all possible information about the activities, aims, and purposes of the organization. It seems altogether creditable that a desire should exist among employees for such information which the best-intentioned executive might think would not interest them and which the worst-intentioned would think was none of their business.

24. The above passage implies that one of the causes of the difficulty which an organization   24.____
    might have with its personnel relations is that its employees

    A. have not expressed interest in the activities, aims, and purposes of the organization
    B. do not believe in the good faith of the organization

C. have not been able to give full cooperation to the organization
D. do not recommend improvements in the practices and policies of the organization

25. According to the above passage, in order for an organization to have good personnel relations, it is NOT essential that 25.___

A. employees have confidence in the organization
B. the purposes of the organization be understood by the employees
C. employees have a desire for information about the organization
D. information about the organization be communicated to employees

———

KEY (CORRECT ANSWERS)

1.	D		11.	D
2.	C		12.	A
3.	D		13.	A
4.	B		14.	C
5.	A		15.	D
6.	A		16.	A
7.	C		17.	D
8.	C		18.	B
9.	A		19.	C
10.	B		20.	D

21.	D
22.	D
23.	A
24.	B
25.	C

———

TEST 2

Questions 1-8.

DIRECTIONS: Questions 1 through 8 are to be answered SOLELY on the basis of the following passage.

Important figures in education and in public affairs have recommended development of a private organization sponsored in part by various private foundations which would offer installment payment plans to full-time matriculated students in accredited colleges and universities in the United States and Canada. Contracts would be drawn to cover either tuition and fees, or tuition, fees, room and board in college facilities, from one year up to and including six years. A special charge, which would vary with the length of the contract, would be added to the gross repayable amount. This would be in addition to interest at a rate which would vary with the income of the parents. There would be a 3% annual interest charge for families with total income, before income taxes, of $50,000 or less. The rate would increase by 1/10 of 1% for every $1,000 of additional net income in excess of $50,000 up to a maximum of 10% interest. Contracts would carry an insurance provision on the life of the parent or guardian who signs the contract; all contracts must have the signature of a parent or guardian. Payment would be scheduled in equal monthly installments.

1. Which of the following students would be eligible for the payment plan described in the above passage? A   1._____

    A. matriculated student taking six semester hours toward a graduate degree
    B. matriculated student taking seventeen semester hours toward an undergraduate degree
    C. graduate matriculated at the University of Mexico taking eighteen semester hours toward a graduate degree
    D. student taking eighteen semester hours in a special pre-matriculation program

2. According to the above passage, the organization described would be sponsored in part by   2._____

    A. private foundations
    B. colleges and universities
    C. persons in the field of education
    D. persons in public life

3. Which of the following expenses could NOT be covered by a contract with the organization described in the above passage?   3._____

    A. Tuition amounting to $20,000 per year
    B. Registration and laboratory fees
    C. Meals at restaurants near the college
    D. Rent for an apartment in a college dormitory

4. The total amount to be paid would include ONLY the   4._____

    A. principal
    B. principal and interest
    C. principal, interest, and special charge
    D. principal, interest, special charge, and fee

5. The contract would carry insurance on the

    A. life of the student
    B. life of the student's parents
    C. income of the parents of the student
    D. life of the parent who signed the contract

6. The interest rate for an annual loan of $25,000 from the organization described in the above passage for a student whose family's net income was $55,000 should be

    A. 3%   B. 3.5%   C. 4%   D. 4.5%

7. The interest rate for an annual loan of $35,000 from the organization described in the above passage for a student whose family's net income was $100,000 should be

    A. 5%   B. 8%   C. 9%   D. 10%

8. John Lee has submitted an application for the installment payment plan described in the above passage. John's mother and father have a store which grossed $500,000 last year, but the income which the family received from the store was $90,000 before taxes. They also had $5,000 income from stock dividends. They paid $10,000 in income taxes. The amount of income upon which the interest should be based is

    A. $85,000   B. $90,000   C. $95,000   D. $105,000

Questions 9-13.

DIRECTIONS: Questions 9 through 13 are to be answered SOLELY on the basis of the following passage.

Since an organization chart is pictorial in nature, there is a tendency for it to be drawn in an artistically balanced and appealing fashion, regardless of the realities of actual organizational structure. In addition to being subject to this distortion, there is the difficulty of communicating in any organization chart the relative importance or the relative size of various component parts of an organizational structure. Furthermore, because of the need for simplicity of design, an organization chart can never indicate the full extent of the interrelationships among the component parts of an organization.

These interrelationships are often just as vital as the specifications which an organization chart endeavors to indicate. Yet, if an organization chart were to be drawn with all the wide variety of criss-crossing communication and cooperation networks existent within a typical organization, the chart would probably be much more confusing than informative. It is also obvious that no organization chart as such can prove or disprove that the organizational structure it represents is effective in realizing the objectives of the organization. At best, an organization chart can only illustrate some of the various factors to be taken into consideration in understanding, devising, or altering organizational arrangements.

9. According to the above passage, an organization chart can be expected to portray the

    A. structure of the organization along somewhat ideal lines
    B. relative size of the organizational units quite accurately
    C. channels of information distribution within the organization graphically
    D. extent of the obligation of each unit to meet the organizational objectives

10. According to the above passage, those aspects of internal functioning which are NOT shown on an organization chart   10.____

    A. can be considered to have little practical application in the operations of the organization
    B. might well be considered to be as important as the structural relationships which a chart does present
    C. could be the cause of considerable confusion in the operations of an organization which is quite large
    D. would be most likely to provide the information needed to determine the overall effectiveness of an organization

11. In the above passage, the one of the following conditions which is NOT implied as being a defect of an organization chart is that an organization chart may   11.____

    A. present a picture of the organizational structure which is different from the structure that actually exists
    B. fail to indicate the comparative size of various organizational units
    C. be limited in its ability to convey some of the meaningful aspects of organizational relationships
    D. become less useful over a period of time during which the organizational facts which it illustrated have changed

12. The one of the following which is the MOST suitable title for the above passage is   12.____

    A. THE DESIGN AND CONSTRUCTION OF AN ORGANIZATION CHART
    B. THE INFORMAL ASPECTS OF AN ORGANIZATION CHART
    C. THE INHERENT DEFICIENCIES OF AN ORGANIZATION CHART
    D. THE UTILIZATION OF A TYPICAL ORGANIZATION CHART

13. It can be INFERRED from the above passage that the function of an organization chart is to   13.____

    A. contribute to the comprehension of the organization form and arrangements
    B. establish the capabilities of the organization to operate effectively
    C. provide a balanced picture of the operations of the organization
    D. eliminate the need for complexity in the organization's structure

Questions 14-16.

DIRECTIONS: Questions 14 through 16 are to be answered SOLELY on the basis of the following passage.

In dealing with visitors to the school office, the school secretary must use initiative, tact, and good judgment. All visitors should be greeted promptly and courteously. The nature of their business should be determined quickly and handled expeditiously. Frequently, the secretary should be able to handle requests, receipts, deliveries, or passes herself. Her judgment should determine when a visitor should see members of the staff or the principal. Serious problems or doubtful cases should be referred to a supervisor.

14. In general, visitors should be handled by the   14.__

    A. school secretary   B. principal
    C. appropriate supervisor   D. person who is free

15. It is wise to obtain the following information from visitors: 15.__

    A. Name   B. Nature of business
    C. Address   D. Problems they have

16. All visitors who wish to see members of the staff should   16.__

    A. be permitted to do so
    B. produce identification
    C. do so for valid reasons only
    D. be processed by a supervisor

Questions 17-19.

DIRECTIONS: Questions 17 through 19 are to be answered SOLELY on the basis of the following passage.

    Information regarding payroll status, salary differentials, promotional salary increments, deductions, and pension payments should be given to all members of the staff who have questions regarding these items. On occasion, if the secretary is uncertain regarding the information, the staff member should be referred to the principal or the appropriate agency. No question by a staff member regarding payroll status should be brushed aside as immaterial or irrelevant. The school secretary must always try to handle the question or pass it on to the person who can handle it.

17. If a teacher is dissatisfied with information regarding her salary status, as given by the   17.__
school secretary, the matter should be

    A. dropped
    B. passed on to the principal
    C. passed on by the secretary to proper agency or the principal
    D. made a basis for grievance procedures

18. The following is an adequate summary of the above passage: 18.__

    A. The secretary must handle all payroll matters
    B. The secretary must handle all payroll matters or know who can handle them
    C. The secretary or the principal must handle all payroll matters
    D. Payroll matters too difficult to handle must be followed up until they are solved

19. The above passage implies that   19.__

    A. many teachers ask immaterial questions regarding payroll status
    B. few teachers ask irrelevant pension questions
    C. no teachers ask immaterial salary questions
    D. no question regarding salary should be considered irrelevant

Questions 20-22.

DIRECTIONS: Questions 20 through 22 are to be answered SOLELY on the basis of the following passage.

The necessity for good speech on the part of the school secretary cannot be overstated.
The school secretary must deal with the general public, the pupils, the members of the staff,
and the school supervisors. In every situation which involves the general public, the secretary
serves as a representative of the school. In dealing with pupils, the secretary's speech must
serve as a model from which students may guide themselves. Slang, colloquialisms, mala-
propisms, and local dialects must be avoided.

20.   The above passage implies that the speech pattern of the secretary must be   20._____

    A.   perfect
    B.   very good
    C.   average
    D.   on a level with that of the pupils

21.   The last sentence indicates that slang   21._____

    A.   is acceptable
    B.   occurs in all speech
    C.   might be used occasionally
    D.   should be shunned

22.   The above passage implies that the speech of pupils   22._____

    A.   may be influenced   B.   does not change readily
    C.   is generally good   D.   is generally poor

Questions 23-25.

DIRECTIONS: Questions 23 through 25 are to be answered SOLELY on the basis of the following passage.

The school secretary who is engaged in the task of filing records and correspondence
should follow a general set of rules. Items which are filed should be available to other secre-
taries or to supervisors quickly and easily by means of the application of a modicum of common sense and good judgment. Items which, by their nature, may be difficult to find should be
cross-indexed. Folders and drawers should be neatly and accurately labeled. There should
never be a large accumulation of papers which have not been filed.

23.   A good general rule to follow in filing is that materials should be   23._____

    A.   placed in folders quickly
    B.   neatly stored
    C.   readily available
    D.   cross-indexed

24.   Items that are filed should be available to   24._____

    A.   the secretary charged with the task of filing
    B.   secretaries and supervisors
    C.   school personnel
    D.   the principal

25. A modicum of common sense means _____ common sense.

    A. an average amount of   B. a great deal of
    C. a little   D. no

25.___

_____

KEY (CORRECT ANSWERS)

1.	B	11.	D
2.	A	12.	C
3.	C	13.	A
4.	C	14.	A
5.	D	15.	B
6.	B	16.	C
7.	B	17.	C
8.	C	18.	B
9.	A	19.	D
10.	B	20.	B

21.	D
22.	A
23.	C
24.	B
25.	C

_____

TEST 3

Questions 1-4.

DIRECTIONS: Questions 1 through 4 are to be answered SOLELY on the basis of the following passage.

The proposition that administrative activity is essentially the same in all organizations appears to underlie some of the practices in the administration of private higher education. Although the practice is unusual in public education, there are numerous instances of industrial, governmental, or military administrators being assigned to private institutions of higher education and, to a lesser extent, of college and university presidents assuming administrative positions in other types of organizations. To test this theory that administrators are interchangeable, there is a need for systematic observation and classification. The myth that an educational administrator must first have experience in the teaching profession is firmly rooted in a long tradition that has historical prestige. The myth is bound up in the expectations of the public and personnel surrounding the administrator. Since administrative success depends significantly on how well an administrator meets the expectations others have of him, the myth may be more powerful than the special experience in helping the administrator attain organizational and educational objectives. Educational administrators who have risen through the teaching profession have often expressed nostalgia for the life of a teacher or scholar, but there is no evidence that this nostalgia contributes to administrative success

1. Which of the following statements as completed is MOST consistent with the above passage? The greatest number of administrators has moved from   1.____

    A.   industry and the military to government and universities
    B.   government and universities to industry and the military
    C.   government, the armed forces, and industry to colleges and universities
    D.   colleges and universities to government, the armed forces, and industry

2. Of the following, the MOST reasonable inference from the above passage is that a specific area requiring further research is the   2.____

    A.   place of myth in the tradition and history of the educational profession
    B.   relative effectiveness of educational administrators from inside and outside the teaching profession
    C.   performance of administrators in the administration of public colleges
    D.   degree of reality behind the nostalgia for scholarly pursuits often expressed by educational administrators

3. According to the above passage, the value to an educational administrator of experience in the teaching profession   3.____

    A.   lies in the firsthand knowledge he has acquired of immediate educational problems
    B.   may lie in the belief of his colleagues, subordinates, and the public that such experience is necessary
    C.   has been supported by evidence that the experience contributes to administrative success in educational fields
    D.   would be greater if the administrator were able to free himself from nostalgia for his former duties

4. Of the following, the MOST suitable title for the above passage is   4.

    A. EDUCATIONAL ADMINISTRATION, ITS PROBLEMS
    B. THE EXPERIENCE NEEDED FOR EDUCATIONAL ADMINISTRATION
    C. ADMINISTRATION IN HIGHER EDUCATION
    D. EVALUATING ADMINISTRATIVE EXPERIENCE

Questions 5-6.

DIRECTIONS: Questions 5 and 6 are to be answered SOLELY on the basis of the following passage.

Management by objectives (MBO) may be defined as the process by which the superior and the subordinate managers of an organization jointly define its common goals, define each individual's major areas of responsibility in terms of the results expected of him and use these measures as guides for operating the unit and assessing the contribution of each of its members.

The MBO approach requires that after organizational goals are established and communicated, targets must be set for each individual position which are congruent with organizational goals. Periodic performance reviews and a final review using the objectives set as criteria are also basic to this approach.

Recent studies have shown that MBO programs are influenced by attitudes and perceptions of the boss, the company, the reward-punishment system, and the program itself. In addition, the manner in which the MBO program is carried out can influence the success of the program. A study done in the late sixties indicates that the best results are obtained when the manager sets goals which deal with significant problem areas in the organizational unit, or with the subordinate's personal deficiencies. These goals must be clear with regard to what is expected of the subordinate. The frequency of feedback is also important in the success of a management-by-objectives program. Generally, the greater the amount of feedback, the more successful the MBO program.

5. According to the above passage, the expected output for individual employees should be determined   5.___

    A. after a number of reviews of work performance
    B. after common organizational goals are defined
    C. before common organizational goals are defined
    D. on the basis of an employee's personal qualities

6. According to the above passage, the management-by-objectives approach requires   6.___

    A. less feedback than other types of management programs
    B. little review of on-the-job performance after the initial setting of goals
    C. general conformance between individual goals and organizational goals
    D. the setting of goals which deal with minor problem areas in the organization

Questions 7-10.

DIRECTIONS: Questions 7 through 10 are to be answered SOLELY on the basis of the following passage.

Management, which is the function of executive leadership, has as its principal phases the planning, organizing, and controlling of the activities of subordinate groups in the accomplishment of organizational objectives. Planning specifies the kind and extent of the factors, forces, and effects, and the relationships among them, that will be required for satisfactory accomplishment. The nature of the objectives and their requirements must be known before determinations can be made as to what must be done, how it must be done and why, where actions should take place, who should be responsible, and similar problems pertaining to the formulation of a plan. Organizing, which creates the conditions that must be present before the execution of the plan can be undertaken successfully, cannot be done intelligently without knowledge of the organizational objectives. Control, which has to do with the constraint and regulation of activities entering into the execution of the plan, must be exercised in accordance with the characteristics and requirements of the activities demanded by the plan.

7. The one of the following which is the MOST suitable title for the above passage is   7.____

    A. THE NATURE OF SUCCESSFUL ORGANIZATION
    B. THE PLANNING OF MANAGEMENT FUNCTIONS
    C. THE IMPORTANCE OF ORGANIZATIONAL FUNCTIONS
    D. THE PRINCIPLE ASPECTS OF MANAGEMENT

8. It can be inferred from the above passage that the one of the following functions whose   8.____
existence is essential to the existence of the other three is the

    A. regulation of the work needed to carry out a plan
    B. understanding of what the organization intends to accomplish
    C. securing of information of the factors necessary for accomplishment of objectives
    D. establishment of the conditions required for successful action

9. The one of the following which would NOT be included within any of the principal phases   9.____
of the function of executive leadership as defined in the above passage is

    A. determination of manpower requirements
    B. procurement of required material
    C. establishment of organizational objectives
    D. scheduling of production

10. The conclusion which can MOST reasonably be drawn from the above passage is that   10.____
the control phase of managing is most directly concerned with the

    A. influencing of policy determinations
    B. administering of suggestion systems
    C. acquisition of staff for the organization
    D. implementation of performance standards

Questions 11-12.

DIRECTIONS: Questions 11 and 12 are to be answered SOLELY on the basis of the following
                passage.

Under an open-and-above-board policy, it is to be expected that some supervisors will gloss over known shortcomings of subordinates rather than face the task of discussing them face-to-face. It is also to be expected that at least some employees whose job performance is below par will reject the supervisor's appraisal as biased and unfair. Be that as it may, these are inescapable aspects of any performance appraisal system in which human beings are involved. The supervisor who shies away from calling a spade a spade, as well as the employee with a chip on his shoulder, will each in his own way eventually be revealed in his true light--to the benefit of the organization as a whole.

11. The BEST of the following interpretations of the above passage is that   11.___

    A.   the method of rating employee performance requires immediate revision to improve employee acceptance
    B.   substandard performance ratings should be discussed with employees even if satisfactory ratings are not
    C.   supervisors run the risk of being called unfair by their subordinates even though their appraisals are accurate
    D.   any system of employee performance rating is satisfactory if used properly

12. The BEST of the following interpretations of the above passage is that   12.___

    A.   supervisors generally are not open-and-above-board with their subordinates
    B.   it is necessary for supervisors to tell employees objectively how they are performing
    C.   employees complain when their supervisor does not keep them informed
    D.   supervisors are afraid to tell subordinates their weaknesses

Questions 13-15.

DIRECTIONS: Questions 13 through 15 are to be answered SOLELY on the basis of the following passage.

During the last decade, a great deal of interest has been generated around the phenomenon of *organizational development,* or the process of developing human resources through conscious organization effort. Organizational development (OD) stresses improving interpersonal relationships and organizational skills, such as communication, to a much greater degree than individual training ever did. The kind of training that an organization should emphasize depends upon the present and future structure of the organization. If future organizations are to be unstable, shifting coalitions, then individual skills and abilities, particularly those emphasizing innovativeness, creativity, flexibility, and the latest technological knowledge, are crucial and individual training is most appropriate.

But if there is to be little change in organizational structure, then the main thrust of training should be group-oriented or organizational development. This approach seems better designed for overcoming hierarchical barriers, for developing a degree of interpersonal relationships which make communication along the chain of command possible, and for retaining a modicum of innovation and/or flexibility.

13. According to the above passage, group-oriented training is MOST useful in   13.___

    A.   developing a communications system that will facilitate understanding through the chain of command
    B.   highly flexible and mobile organizations
    C.   preventing the crossing of hierarchical barriers within an organization
    D.   saving energy otherwise wasted on developing methods of dealing with rigid hierarchies

14. The one of the following conclusions which can be drawn MOST appropriately from the
above passage is that

    A. behavioral research supports the use of organizational development training methods rather than individualized training
    B. it is easier to provide individualized training in specific skills than to set up sensitivity training programs
    C. organizational development eliminates innovative or flexible activity
    D. the nature of an organization greatly influences which training methods will be most effective

14._____

15. According to the above passage, the one of the following which is LEAST important for
large-scale organizations geared to rapid and abrupt change is

    A. current technological information
    B. development of a high degree of interpersonal relationships
    C. development of individual skills and abilities
    D. emphasis on creativity

15._____

Questions 16-18.

DIRECTIONS: Questions 16 through 18 are to be answered SOLELY on the basis of the following passage.

    The increase in the extent to which each individual is personally responsible to others is most noticeable in a large bureaucracy. No one person *decides* anything; each decision of any importance, is the product of an intricate process of brokerage involving individuals inside and outside the organization who feel some reason to be affected by the decision, or who have special knowledge to contribute to it. The more varied the organization's constituency, the more outside *veto-groups* will need to be taken into account. But even if no outside consultations were involved, sheer size would produce a complex process of decision. For a large organization is a deliberately created system of tensions into which each individual is expected to bring work-ways, viewpoints, and outside relationships markedly different from those of his colleagues. It is the administrator's task to draw from these disparate forces the elements of wise action from day to day, consistent with the purposes of the organization as a whole.

16. The above passage is essentially a description of decision making as

    A. an organization process
    B. the key responsibility of the administrator
    C. the one best position among many
    D. a complex of individual decisions

16._____

17. Which one of the following statements BEST describes the responsibilities of an administrator?

    A. He modifies decisions and goals in accordance with pressures from within and outside the organization.
    B. He creates problem-solving mechanisms that rely on the varied interests of his staff and *veto-groups.*
    C. He makes determinations that will lead to attainment of his agency's objectives.
    D. He obtains agreement among varying viewpoints and interests.

17._____

18. In the context of the operations of a central public personnel agency, a *veto group* would LEAST likely consist of

    A. employee organizations
    B. professional personnel societies
    C. using agencies
    D. civil service newspapers

Questions 19-25.

DIRECTIONS: Questions 19 through 25 are to be answered SOLELY on the basis of the following passage, which is an extract from a report prepared for Department X, which outlines the procedure to be followed in the case of transfers of employees.

Every transfer, regardless of the reason therefore, requires completion of the record of transfer, Form DT 411. To denote consent to the transfer, DT 411 should contain the signatures of the transferee and the personnel officer(s) concerned, except that, in the case of an involuntary transfer, the signatures of the transferee's present and prospective supervisors shall be entered in Boxes 8A and 8B, respectively, since the transferee does not consent. Only a permanent employee may request a transfer; in such cases, the employee's attendance record shall be duly considered with regard to absences, latenesses, and accrued overtime balances. In the case of an inter-district transfer, the employee's attendance record must be included in Section 8A of the transfer request, Form DT 410, by the personnel officer of the district from which the transfer is requested. The personnel officer of the district to which the employee requested transfer may refuse to accept accrued overtime balances in excess of ten days.

An employee on probation shall be eligible for transfer. If such employee is involuntarily transferred, he shall be credited for the period of time already served on probation. However, if such transfer is voluntary, the employee shall be required to serve the entire period of his probation in the new position. An employee who has occurred a disability which prevents him from performing his normal duties may be transferred during the period of such disability to other appropriate duties. A disability transfer requires the completion of either Form DT 414 if the disability is job-connected, or Form DT 415 if it is not a job-connected disability. In either case, the personnel officer of the district from which the transfer is made signs in Box 6A of the first two copies and the personnel officer of the district to which the transfer is made signs in Box 6B of the last two copies, or, in the case of an intra-district disability transfer, the personnel officer must sign in Box 6A of the first two copies and Box 6B of the last two copies.

19. When a personnel officer consents to an employee's request for transfer from his district, this procedure requires that the personnel officer sign Form(s)

    A. DT 411
    B. DT 410 and DT 411
    C. DT 411 and either Form DT 414 or DT 415
    D. DT 410 and DT 411, and either Form DT 414 or DT 415

20. With respect to the time record of an employee transferred against his wishes during his probationary period, this procedure requires that

    A. he serve the entire period of his probation in his present office
    B. he lose his accrued overtime balance

C.   his attendance record be considered with regard to absences and latenesses
D.   he be given credit for the period of time he has already served on probation

21.   Assume you are a supervisor and an employee must be transferred into your office   21._____
against his wishes. According to the this procedure, the box you must sign on the record
of transfer is

A. 6A   B. 8A   C. 6B   D. 8B

22.   Under this procedure, in the case of a disability transfer, when must Box 6A on Forms DT   22._____
414 and DT 415 be signed by the personnel officer of the district to which the transfer is
being made?

A.   In all cases when either Form DT 414 or Form DT 415 is used
B.   In all cases when Form DT 414 is used and only under certain circumstances
when Form DT 415 is used
C.   In all cases when Form DT 415 is used and only under certain circumstances
when Form DT 414 is used
D.   Only under certain circumstances when either Form DT 414 or Form DT 415 is
used

23.   From the above passage, it may be inferred MOST correctly that the number of copies of   23._____
Form DT 414 is

A.   no more than 2
B.   at least 3
C.   at least 5
D.   more than the number of copies of Form DT 415

24.   A change in punctuation and capitalization only which would change one sentence into   24._____
two and possibly contribute to somewhat greater ease of reading this report extract
would be MOST appropriate in the

A.   2nd sentence, 1st paragraph
B.   3rd sentence, 1st paragraph
C.   next to he last sentence, 2nd paragraph
D.   2nd sentence, 2nd paragraph

25.   In the second paragraph, a word that is INCORRECTLY used is   25._____

A.   *shall* in the 1st sentence
B.   *voluntary* in the 3rd sentence
C.   *occurred* in the 4th sentence
D.   *intra-district* in the last sentence

KEY (CORRECT ANSWERS)

1.	C		11.	C
2.	B		12.	B
3.	B		13.	A
4.	B		14.	D
5.	B		15.	B
6.	C		16.	A
7.	D		17.	C
8.	B		18.	B
9.	C		19.	A
10.	D		20.	D

21.	D
22.	D
23.	B
24.	B
25.	C

PHILOSOPHY, PRINCIPLES, PRACTICES, AND TECHNICS
OF
SUPERVISION, ADMINISTRATION, MANAGEMENT, AND ORGANIZATION

CONTENTS

CONTENTS (cont'd)

PHILOSOPHY, PRINCIPLES, PRACTICES, AND TECHNICS
OF
SUPERVISION, ADMINISTRATION, MANAGEMENT, AND ORGANIZATION

I. MEANING OF SUPERVISION

The extension of the democratic philosophy has been accompanied by an extension in the scope of supervision. Modern leaders and supervisors no longer think of supervision in the narrow sense of being confined chiefly to visiting employees, supplying materials, or rating the staff. They regard supervision as being intimately related to all the concerned agencies of society, they speak of the supervisor's function in terms of "growth", rather than the "improvement," of employees

This modern concept of supervision may be defined as follows:

Supervision is leadership and the development of leadership within groups which are cooperatively engaged in inspection, research, training, guidance and evaluation.

II. THE OLD AND THE NEW SUPERVISION

TRADITIONAL	*MODERN*
1. Inspection	1. Study and analysis
2. Focused on the employee	2. Focused on aims, materials, methods, supervisors, employees, environment
3. Visitation	3. Demonstrations, intervisitation, workshops, directed reading, bulletins, etc.
4. Random and haphazard	4. Definitely organized and planned (scientific)
5. Imposed and authoritarian	5. Cooperative and democratic
6. One person usually	6. Many persons involved (creative)

III. THE EIGHT (8) BASIC PRINCIPLES OF THE NEW SUPERVISION

1. *PRINCIPLE OF RESPONSIBILITY*

   Authority to act and responsibility for acting must be joined.
   a. If you give responsibility, give authority.
   b. Define employee duties clearly.
   c. Protect employees from criticism by others.
   d. Recognize the rights as well as obligations of employees.
   e. Achieve the aims of a democratic society insofar as it is possible within the area of your work.
   f. Establish a situation favorable to training and learning.
   g. Accept ultimate responsibility for everything done in your section, unit, office, division, department.
   h. Good administration and good supervision are inseparable.

2. *PRINCIPLE OF AUTHORITY*

   The success of the supervisor is measured by the extent to which the power of authority is not used.
   a. Exercise simplicity and informality in supervision.
   b. Use the simplest machinery of supervision.
   c. If it is good for the organization as a whole, it is probably justified.
   d. Seldom be arbitrary or authoritative.
   e. Do not base your work on the power of position or of personality.
   f. Permit and encourage the free expression of opinions.

3. *PRINCIPLE OF SELF-GROWTH*

   The success of the supervisor is measured by the extent to which, and the speed with which, he is no longer needed.
   a. Base criticism on principles, not on specifics.
   b. Point out higher activities to employees.

    c. Train for self-thinking by employees, to meet new situations.
    d. Stimulate initiative, self-reliance and individual responsibility.
    e. Concentrate on stimulating the growth of employees rather than on removing defects.

4. *PRINCIPLE OF INDIVIDUAL WORTH*
    Respect for the individual is a paramount consideration in supervision.
    a. Be human and sympathetic in dealing with employees.
    b. Don't nag about things to be done.
    c. Recognize the individual differences among employees and seek opportunities to permit best expression of each personality.

5. *PRINCIPLE OF CREATIVE LEADERSHIP*
    The best supervision is that which is not apparent to the employee.
    a. Stimulate, don't drive employees to creative action.
    b. Emphasize doing good things.
    c. Encourage employees to do what they do best.
    d. Do not be too greatly concerned with details of subject or method.
    e. Do not be concerned exclusively with immediate problems and activities.
    f. Reveal higher activities and make them both desired and maximally possible.
    g. Determine procedures in the light of each situation but see that these are derived from a sound basic philosophy.
    h. Aid, inspire and lead so as to liberate the creative spirit latent in all good employees.

6. *PRINCIPLE OF SUCCESS AND FAILURE*
    There are no unsuccessful employees, only unsuccessful supervisors who have failed to give proper leadership.
    a. Adapt suggestions to the capacities, attitudes, and prejudices of employees.
    b. Be gradual, be progressive, be persistent.
    c. Help the employee find the general principle; have the employee apply his own problem to the general principle.
    d. Give adequate appreciation for good work and honest effort.
    e. Anticipate employee difficulties and help to prevent them.
    f. Encourage employees to do the desirable things they will do anyway.
    g. Judge your supervision by the results it secures.

7. *PRINCIPLE OF SCIENCE*
    Successful supervision is scientific, objective, and experimental. It is based on facts, not on prejudices.
    a. Be cumulative in results.
    b. Never divorce your suggestions from the goals of training.
    c. Don't be impatient of results.
    d. Keep all matters on a professional, not a personal level.
    e. Do not be concerned exclusively with immediate problems and activities.
    f. Use objective means of determining achievement and rating where possible.

8. *PRINCIPLE OF COOPERATION*
    Supervision is a cooperative enterprise between supervisor and employee.
    a. Begin with conditions as they are.
    b. Ask opinions of all involved when formulating policies.

        c. Organization is as good as its weakest link.
        d. Let employees help to determine policies and department
           programs.
        e. Be approachable and accessible - physically and mentally.
        f. Develop pleasant social relationships.
IV. WHAT IS ADMINISTRATION?
        Administration is concerned with providing the environment, the
    material facilities, and the operational procedures that will promote
    the maximum growth and development of supervisors and employees. (Or-
    ganization is an aspect, and a concomitant, of administration.)
        There is no sharp line of demarcation between supervision and ad-
    ministration; these functions are intimately interrelated and, often,
    overlapping. They are complementary activities.
        1. *PRACTICES COMMONLY CLASSED AS "SUPERVISORY"*
            a. Conducting employees conferences
            b. Visiting sections, units, offices, divisions, departments
            c. Arranging for demonstrations
            d. Examining plans
            e. Suggesting professional reading
            f. Interpreting bulletins
            g. Recommending in-service training courses
            h. Encouraging experimentation
            i. Appraising employee morale
            j. Providing for intervisitation
        2. *PRACTICES COMMONLY CLASSIFIED AS "ADMINISTRATIVE"*
            a. Management of the office
            b. Arrangement of schedules for extra duties
            c. Assignment of rooms or areas
            d. Distribution of supplies
            e. Keeping records and reports
            f. Care of audio-visual materials
            g. Keeping inventory records
            h. Checking record cards and books
            i. Programming special activities
            j. Checking on the attendance and punctuality of employees
        3. *PRACTICES COMMONLY CLASSIFIED AS BOTH "SUPERVISORY" AND
           "ADMINISTRATIVE"*
            a. Program construction
            b. Testing or evaluating outcomes
            c. Personnel accounting
            d. Ordering instructional materials
V. RESPONSIBILITIES OF THE SUPERVISOR
        A person employed in a supervisory capacity must constantly be
    able to improve his own efficiency and ability. He represents the
    employer to the employees and only continuous self-examination can
    make him a capable supervisor.
        Leadership and training are the supervisor's responsibility. An
    efficient working unit is one in which the employees work with the
    supervisor. It is his job to bring out the best in his employees.
    He must always be relaxed, courteous and calm in his association with
    his employees. Their feelings are important, and a harsh attitude
    does not develop the most efficient employees.

VI. COMPETENCIES OF THE SUPERVISOR
1. Complete knowledge of the duties and responsibilities of his position.
2. To be able to organize a job, plan ahead and carry through.
3. To have self-confidence and initiative.
4. To be able to handle the unexpected situation and make quick decisions.
5. To be able to properly train subordinates in the positions they are best suited for.
6. To be able to keep good human relations among his subordinates.
7. To be able to keep good human relations between his subordinates and himself and to earn their respect and trust.

VII. THE PROFESSIONAL SUPERVISOR-EMPLOYEE RELATIONSHIP

There are two kinds of efficiency: one kind is only apparent and is produced in organizations through the exercise of mere discipline; this is but a simulation of the second, or true, efficiency which springs from spontaneous cooperation. If you are a manager, no matter how great or small your responsibility, it is your job, in the final analysis, to create and develop this involuntary cooperation among the people whom you supervise. For, no matter how powerful a combination of money, machines, and materials a company may have, this is a dead and sterile thing without a team of willing, thinking and articulate people to guide it.

The following 21 points are presented as indicative of the exemplary basic relationship that should exist between supervisor and employee:

1. Each person wants to be liked and respected by his fellow employee and wants to be treated with consideration and respect by his superior.
2. The most competent employee will make an error. However, in a unit where good relations exist between the supervisor and his employees, tenseness and fear do not exist. Thus, errors are not hidden or covered up and the efficiency of a unit is not impaired.
3. Subordinates resent rules, regulations, or orders that are unreasonable or unexplained.
4. Subordinates are quick to resent unfairness, harshness, injustices and favoritism.
5. An employee will accept responsibility if he knows that he will be complimented for a job well done, and not too harshly chastized for failure; that his supervisor will check the cause of the failure, and, if it was the supervisor's fault, he will assume the blame therefor. If it was the employee's fault, his supervisor will explain the correct method or means of handling the responsibility.
6. An employee wants to receive credit for a suggestion he has made, that is used. If a suggestion cannot be used, the employee is entitled to an explanation. The supervisor should not say "no" and close the subject.
7. Fear and worry slow up a worker's ability. Poor working environment can impair his physical and mental health. A good supervisor avoids forceful methods, threats and arguments to get a job done.
8. A forceful supervisor is able to train his employees individually and as a team, and is able to motivate them in the proper channels.

4

9. A mature supervisor is able to properly evaluate his subordinates and to keep them happy and satisfied.
10. A sensitive supervisor will never patronize his subordinates.
11. A worthy supervisor will respect his employees' confidences.
12. Definite and clear-cut responsibilities should be assigned to each executive.
13. Responsibility should always be coupled with corresponding authority.
14. No change should be made in the scope or responsibilities of a position without a definite understanding to that effect on the part of all persons concerned.
15. No executive or employee, occupying a single position in the organization, should be subject to definite orders from more than one source.
16. Orders should never be given to subordinates over the head of a responsible executive. Rather than do this, the officer in question should be supplanted.
17. Criticisms of subordinates should, whever possible, be made privately, and in no case should a subordinate be criticized in the presence of executives or employees of equal or lower rank.
18. No dispute or difference between executives or employees as to authority or responsibilities should be considered too trivial for prompt and careful adjudication.
19. Promotions, wage changes, and disciplinary action should always be approved by the executive immediately superior to the one directly responsible.
20. No executive or employee should ever be required, or expected, to be at the same time an assistant to, and critic of, another.
21. Any executive whose work is subject to regular inspection should, whever practicable, be given the assistance and facilities necessary to enable him to maintain an independent check of the quality of his work.

VIII. MINI-TEXT IN SUPERVISION, ADMINISTRATION, MANAGEMENT, AND ORGANIZATION
A. BRIEF HIGHLIGHTS
Listed concisely and sequentially are major headings and important data in the field for quick recall and review.
1. *LEVELS OF MANAGEMENT*
   Any organization of some size has several levels of management. In terms of a ladder the levels are:

The first level is very important because it is the beginning point of management leadership.
2. *WHAT THE SUPERVISOR MUST LEARN*
   A supervisor must learn to:
   (1) Deal with people and their differences
   (2) Get the job done through people
   (3) Recognize the problems when they exist
   (4) Overcome obstacles to good performance
   (5) Evaluate the performance of people
   (6) Check his own performance in terms of accomplishment

3. *A DEFINITION OF SUPERVISOR*
   The term supervisor means any individual having authority, in the interests of the employer, to hire,transfer,suspend,lay-off,recall, promote,discharge,assign,reward,or discipline other employees... or responsibility to direct them,or to adjust their grievances,or effectively to recommend such action,if, in connection with the foregoing, exercise of such authority is not of a merely routine or clerical nature but requires the use of independent judgment.

4. *ELEMENTS OF THE TEAM CONCEPT*
   What is involved in teamwork? The component parts are:

(1) Members	(3) Goals	(5) Cooperation
(2) A leader	(4) Plans	(6) Spirit

5. *PRINCIPLES OF ORGANIZATION*
   (1) A team member must know what his job is
   (2) Be sure that the nature and scope of a job are understood
   (3) Authority and responsibility should be carefully spelled out
   (4) A supervisor should be permitted to make the maximum number of decisions affecting his employees
   (5) Employees should report to only one supervisor
   (6) A supervisor should direct only as many employees as he can handle effectively
   (7) An organization plan should be flexible
   (8) Inspection and performance of work should be separate
   (9) Organizational problems should receive immediate attention
   (10) Assign work in line with ability and experience

6. *THE FOUR IMPORTANT PARTS OF EVERY JOB*
   (1) Inherent in every job is the *accountability* for results
   (2) A second set of factors in every job are *responsibilities*
   (3) Along with duties and responsibilities one must have the *authority* to act within certain limits without obtaining permission to proceed
   (4) No job exists in a vacuum. The supervisor is surrounded by key *relationships*

7. *PRINCIPLES OF DELEGATION*
   Where work is delegated for the first time,the supervisor should think in terms of these questions:
   (1) Who is best qualified to do this?
   (2) Can an employee improve his abilities by doing this?
   (3) How long should an employee spend on this?
   (4) Are there any special problems for which he will need guidance?
   (5) How broad a delegation can I make?

8. *PRINCIPLES OF EFFECTIVE COMMUNICATIONS*
   (1) Determine the media
   (2) To whom directed?
   (3) Identification and source authority
   (4) Is communication understood?

9. *PRINCIPLES OF WORK IMPROVEMENT*
   (1) Most people usually do only the work which is assigned to them
   (2) Workers are likely to fit assigned work into the time available to perform it
   (3) A good workload usually stimulates output
   (4) People usually do their best work when they know that results will be reviewed or inspected

(5) Employees usually feel that someone else is responsible for conditions of work, workplace layout, job methods, type of tools and equipment, and other such factors

(6) Employees are usually defensive about their job security

(7) Employees have natural resistance to change

(8) Employees can support or destroy a supervisor

(9) A supervisor usually earns the respect of his people through his personal example of diligence and efficiency

10. *AREAS OF JOB IMPROVEMENT*

The *areas* of job improvement are quite numerous, but the most common ones which a supervisor can identify and utilize are:

(1) Departmental layout
(2) Flow of work
(3) Workplace layout
(4) Utilization of manpower
(5) Work methods
(6) Materials handling
(7) Utilization
(8) Motion economy

11. *SEVEN KEY POINTS IN MAKING IMPROVEMENTS*

(1) Select the job to be improved
(2) Study how it is being done now
(3) Question the present method
(4) Determine actions to be taken
(5) Chart proposed method
(6) Get approval and apply
(7) Solicit worker participation

12. *CORRECTIVE TECHNIQUES OF JOB IMPROVEMENT*

Specific Problems	*General Problems*	*Corrective Technique*
(1) Size of workload	(1) Departmental layout	(1) Study with scale model
(2) Inability to meet schedules	(2) Flow of work	(2) Flow chart study
(3) Strain and fatigue	(3) Workplan layout	(3) Motion analysis
(4) Improper use of men and skills	(4) Utilization of manpower	(4) Comparison of units produced to standard allowances
(5) Waste, poor quality, unsafe conditions	(5) Work methods	(5) Methods analysis
(6) Bottleneck conditions that hinder output	(6) Materials handling	(6) Flow chart and equipment study
(7) Poor utilization of equipment and machines	(7) Utilization of equipment	(7) Down time vs. running time
(8) Efficiency and productivity of labor	(8) Motion economy	(8) Motion analysis

13. *A PLANNING CHECKLIST*

(1) Objectives
(2) Controls
(3) Delegations
(4) Communications
(5) Resources
(6) Methods and procedures
(7) Manpower
(8) Equipment
(9) Supplies and materials
(10) Utilization of time
(11) Safety
(12) Money
(13) Work
(14) Timing of improvements

14. *FIVE CHARACTERISTICS OF GOOD DIRECTIONS*

In order to get results, directions must be:

(1) Possible of accomplishment
(2) Agreeable with worker interests
(3) Related to mission
(4) Planned and complete
(5) Unmistakably clear

15. *TYPES OF DIRECTIONS*
      (1) Demands or direct orders.   (3) Suggestion or implication
      (2) Requests   (4) Volunteering

16. *CONTROLS*
    A typical listing of the overall areas in which the supervisor should establish controls might be:
      (1) Manpower   (4) Quantity of work   (7) Money
      (2) Materials   (5) Time   (8) Methods
      (3) Quality of work   (6) Space

17. *ORIENTING THE NEW EMPLOYEE*
      (1) Prepare for him   (3) Orientation for the job
      (2) Welcome the new employee   (4) Follow-up

18. *CHECKLIST FOR ORIENTING NEW EMPLOYEES*

                                             Yes No

      (1) Do your appreciate the feelings of new employees when they first report for work? ... ...
      (2) Are you aware of the fact that the new employee must make a big adjustment to his job? ... ...
      (3) Have you given him good reasons for liking the job and the organization? ... ...
      (4) Have you prepared for his first day on the job? ... ...
      (5) Did you welcome him cordially and make him feel needed? ... ...
      (6) Did you establish rapport with him so that he feels free to talk and discuss matters with you? ... ...
      (7) Did you explain his job to him and his relationship to you? ... ...
      (8) Does he know that his work will be evaluated periodically on a basis that is fair and objective? ... ...
      (9) Did you introduce him to his fellow workers in such a way that they are likely to accept him? ... ...
    (10) Does he know what employee benefits he will receive? ... ...
    (11) Does he understand the importance of being on the job and what to do if he must leave his duty station? ... ...
    (12) Has he been impressed with the importance of accident prevention and safe practice? ... ...
    (13) Does he generally know his way around the department? ... ...
    (14) Is he under the guidance of a sponsor who will teach the right ways of doing things? ... ...
    (15) Do you plan to follow-up so that he will continue to adjust successfully to his job? ... ...

19. *PRINCIPLES OF LEARNING*
      (1) Motivation   (2) Demonstration or explanation
      (3) Practice

20. *CAUSES OF POOR PERFORMANCE*
      (1) Improper training for job   (6) Lack of standards of
      (2) Wrong tools   performance
      (3) Inadequate directions   (7) Wrong work habits
      (4) Lack of supervisory follow-up(8) Low morale
      (5) Poor communications   (9) Other

21. *FOUR MAJOR STEPS IN ON-THE-JOB INSTRUCTION*
      (1) Prepare the worker   (3) Tryout performance
      (2) Present the operation   (4) Follow-up

22. *EMPLOYEES WANT FIVE THINGS*
      (1) Security   (2) Opportunity (3) Recognition
      (4) Inclusion   (5) Expression
23. *SOME DON'TS IN REGARD TO PRAISE*
      (1) Don't praise a person for something he hasn't done
      (2) Don't praise a person unless you can be sincere
      (3) Don't be sparing in praise just because your superior
           withholds it from you
      (4) Don't let too much time elapse between good performance
           and recognition of it
24. *HOW TO GAIN YOUR WORKERS' CONFIDENCE*
    Methods of developing confidence include such things as:
      (1) Knowing the interests, habits, hobbies of employees
      (2) Admitting your own inadequacies
      (3) Sharing and telling of confidence in others
      (4) Supporting people when they are in trouble
      (5) Delegating matters that can be well handled
      (6) Being frank and straightforward about problems and work-
           ing conditions
      (7) Encouraging others to bring their problems to you
      (8) Taking action on problems which impede worker progress
25. *SOURCES OF EMPLOYEE PROBLEMS*
    On-the-job causes might be such things as:
      (1) A feeling that favoritism is exercised in assignments
      (2) Assignment of overtime
      (3) An undue amount of supervision
      (4) Changing methods or systems
      (5) Stealing of ideas or trade secrets
      (6) Lack of interest in job
      (7) Threat of reduction in force
      (8) Ignorance or lack of communications
      (9) Poor equipment
    (10) Lack of knowing how supervisor feels toward employee
    (11) Shift assignments
    Off-the-job problems might have to do with:
      (1) Health (2) Finances (3) Housing (4) Family
26. *THE SUPERVISOR'S KEY TO DISCIPLINE*
    There are several key points about discipline which the super-
visor should keep in mind:
      (1) Job discipline is one of the disciplines of life and is
           directed by the supervisor.
      (2) It is more important to correct an employee fault than to
           fix blame for it.
      (3) Employee performance is affected by problems both on the
           job and off.
      (4) Sudden or abrupt changes in behavior can be indications of
           important employee problems.
      (5) Problems should be dealt with as soon as possible after
           they are identified.
      (6) The attitude of the supervisor may have more to do with
           solving problems than the techniques of problem solving.
      (7) Correction of employee behavior should be resorted to only
           after the supervisor is sure that training or counseling
           will not be helpful
      (8) Be sure to document your disciplinary actions.

   (9) Make sure that you are disciplining on the basis of facts rather than personal feelings.

  (10) Take each disciplinary step in order, being careful not to make snap judgments, or decisions based on impatience.

27. *FIVE IMPORTANT PROCESSES OF MANAGEMENT*

   (1) Planning   (2) Organizing   (3) Scheduling

   (4) Controlling (5) Motivating

28. *WHEN THE SUPERVISOR FAILS TO PLAN*

   (1) Supervisor creates impression of not knowing his job

   (2) May lead to excessive overtime

   (3) Job runs itself-- supervisor lacks control

   (4) Deadlines and appointments missed

   (5) Parts of the work go undone

   (6) Work interrupted by emergencies

   (7) Sets a bad example

   (8) Uneven workload creates peaks and valleys

   (9) Too much time on minor details at expense of more important tasks

29. *FOURTEEN GENERAL PRINCIPLES OF MANAGEMENT*

   (1) Division of work   (8) Centralization

   (2) Authority and responsibility (9) Scalar chain

   (3) Discipline   (10) Order

   (4) Unity of command   (11) Equity

   (5) Unity of direction   (12) Stability of tenure of

   (6) Subordination of individual personnel

     interest to general interest(13) Initiative

   (7) Remuneration of personnel (14) Esprit de corps

30. *CHANGE*

  Bringing about change is perhaps attempted more often, and yet less well understood, than anything else the supervisor does. How do people generally react to change? (People tend to resist change that is imposed upon them by other individuals or circumstances.)

  Change is characteristic of every situation. It is a part of **every** real endeavor where the efforts of people are concerned.

  A. Why do people resist change?

   People may resist change because of:

    (1) Fear of the unknown

    (2) Implied criticism

    (3) Unpleasant experiences in the past

    (4) Fear of loss of status

    (5) Threat to the ego

    (6) Fear of loss of economic stability

  B. How can we best overcome the resistance to change?

   In initiating change, take these steps:

    (1) Get ready to sell

    (2) identify sources of help

    (3) Anticipate objections

    (4) Sell benefits

    (5) Listen in depth

    (6) Follow up

B. BRIEF TOPICAL SUMMARIES

I. WHO/WHAT IS THE SUPERVISOR?
1. The supervisor is often called the "highest level employee and the lowest level manager."
2. A supervisor is a member of both management and the work group. He acts as a bridge between the two.
3. Most problems in supervision are in the area of human relations, or people problems.
4. Employees expect: Respect, opportunity to learn and to advance, and a sense of belonging, and so forth.
5. Supervisors are responsible for directing people and organizing work. Planning is of paramount importance.
6. A position description is a set of duties and responsibilities inherent to a given position.
7. It is important to keep the position description up-to-date and to provide each employee with his own copy.

II. THE SOCIOLOGY OF WORK
1. People are alike in many ways; however each individual is unique.
2. The supervisor is challenged in getting to know employee differences. Acquiring skills in evaluating individuals is an asset.
3. Maintaining meaningful working relationships in the organization is of great importance.
4. The supervisor has an obligation to help individuals to develop to their fullest potential.
5. Job rotation on a planned basis helps to build versatility and to maintain interest and enthusiasm in work groups.
6. Cross training (job rotation) provides backup skills.
7. The supervisor can help reduce tension by maintaining a sense of humor, providing guidance to employees, and by making reasonable and timely decisions. Employees respond favorably to working under reasonably predictable circumstances.
8. Change is characteristic of all managerial behavior. The supervisor must adjust to changes in procedures, new methods, technological changes, and to a number of new and sometimes challenging situations.
9. To overcome the natural tendency for people to resist change, the supervisor should become more skillful in initiating change.

III. PRINCIPLES AND PRACTICES OF SUPERVISION
1. Employees should be required to answer to only one superior.
2. A supervisor can effectively direct only a limited number of employees, depending upon the complexity, variety, and proximity of the jobs involved.
3. The organizational chart presents the organization in graphic form. It reflects lines of authority and responsibility as well as interrelationships of units within the organization.
4. Distribution of work can be improved through an analysis using the "Work Distribution Chart."
5. The "Work Distribution Chart" reflects the division of work within a unit in understandable form.
6. When related tasks are given to an employee, he has a better chance of increasing his skills through training.
7. The individual who is given the responsibility for tasks must also be given the appropriate authority to insure adequate results.
8. The supervisor should delegate repetitive, routine work. Preparation of recurring reports, maintaining leave and attendance records are some examples.

9. Good discipline is essential to good task performance. Discipline is reflected in the actions of employees on the job in the absence of supervision.
10. Disciplinary action may have to be taken when the positive aspects of discipline have failed. Reprimand, warning, and suspension are examples of disciplinary action.
11. If a situation calls for a reprimand, be sure it is deserved and remember it is to be done in private.

IV. DYNAMIC LEADERSHIP

1. A style is a personal method or manner of exerting influence.
2. Authoritarian leaders often see themselves as the source of power and authority.
3. The democratic leader often perceives the group as the source of authority and power.
4. Supervisors tend to do better when using the pattern of leadership that is most natural for them.
5. Social scientists suggest that the effective supervisor use the leadership style that best fits the problem or circumstances involved.
6. All four styles -- telling, selling, consulting, joining -- have their place. Using one does not preclude using the other at another time.
7. The theory X point of view assumes that the average person dislikes work, will avoid it whenever possible, and must be coerced to achieve organizational objectives.
8. The theory Y point of view assumes that the average person considers work to be as natural as play, and, when the individual is committed, he requires little supervision or direction to accomplish desired objectives.
9. The leader's basic assumptions concerning human behavior and human nature affect his actions, decisions, and other managerial practices.
10. Dissatisfaction among employees is often present, but difficult to isolate. The supervisor should seek to weaken dissatisfaction by keeping promises, being sincere and considerate, keeping employees informed, and so forth.
11. Constructive suggestions should be encouraged during the natural progress of the work.

V. PROCESSES FOR SOLVING PROBLEMS

1. People find their daily tasks more meaningful and satisfying when they can improve them.
2. The causes of problems, or the key factors, are often hidden in the background. Ability to solve problems often involves the ability to isolate them from their backgrounds. There is some substance to the cliché that some persons "can't see the forest for the trees."
3. New procedures are often developed from old ones. Problems should be broken down into manageable parts. New ideas can be adapted from old ones.
4. People think differently in problem-solving situations. Using a logical, patterned approach is often useful. One approach found to be useful includes these steps:

    (a) Define the problem   (d) Weigh and decide
    (b) Establish objectives   (e) Take action
    (c) Get the facts   (f) Evaluate action

VI. TRAINING FOR RESULTS

1. Participants respond best when they feel training is important to them.
2. The supervisor has responsibility for the training and development of those who report to him.
3. When training is delegated to others, great care must be exercised to insure the trainer has knowledge, aptitude, and interest for his work as a trainer.
4. Training (learning) of some type goes on continually. The most successful supervisor makes certain the learning contributes in a productive manner to operational goals.
5. New employees are particularly susceptible to training. Older employees facing new job situations require specific training, as well as having need for development and growth opportunities.
6. Training needs require continuous monitoring.
7. The training officer of an agency is a professional with a responsibility to assist supervisors in solving training problems.
8. Many of the self-development steps important to the supervisor's own growth are equally important to the development of peers and subordinates. Knowledge of these is important when the supervisor consults with others on development and growth opportunities.

VII. HEALTH, SAFETY, AND ACCIDENT PREVENTION

1. Management-minded supervisors take appropriate measures to assist employees in maintaining health and in assuring safe practices in the work environment.
2. Effective safety training and practices help to avoid injury and accidents.
3. Safety should be a management goal. All infractions of safety which are observed should be corrected without exception.
4. Employees' safety attitude, training and instruction, provision of safe tools and equipment, supervision, and leadership are considered highly important factors which contribute to safety and which can be influenced directly by supervisors.
5. When accidents do occur they should be investigated promptly for very important reasons, including the fact that information which is gained can be used to prevent accidents in the future.

VIII. EQUAL EMPLOYMENT OPPORTUNITY

1. The supervisor should endeavor to treat all employees fairly, without regard to religion, race, sex, or national origin.
2. Groups tend to reflect the attitude of the leader. Prejudice can be detected even in very subtle form. Supervisors must strive to create a feeling of mutual respect and confidence in every employee.
3. Complete utilization of all human resources is a national goal. Equitable consideration should be accorded women in the work force, minority-group members, the physically and mentally handicapped, and the older employee. The important question is: "Who can do the job?"
4. Training opportunities, recognition for performance, overtime assignments, promotional opportunities, and all other personnel actions are to be handled on an equitable basis.

IX. IMPROVING COMMUNICATIONS

1. Communications is achieving understanding between the sender and the receiver of a message. It also means sharing information -- the creation of understanding.
2. Communication is basic to all human activity. Words are means of conveying meanings; however, real meanings are in people.
3. There are very practical differences in the effectiveness of one way, impersonal, and two-way communications. Words spoken face-to-face are better understood. Telephone conversations are effective, but lack the rapport of person-to-person exchanges. The whole person communicates.
4. Cooperation and communication in an organization go hand-in-hand. When there is a mutual respect between people, spelling out rules and procedures for communicating is unnecessary.
5. There are several barriers to effective communications. These include failure to listen with respect and understanding, lack of skill in feedback, and misinterpreting the meanings of words used by the speaker. It is also common practice to listen to what we want to hear, and tune out things we do not want to hear.
6. Communication is management's chief problem. The supervisor should accept the challenge to communicate more effectively and to improve interagency and intra-agency communications.
7. The supervisor may often plan for and conduct meetings. The planning phase is critical and may determine the success or the failure of a meeting.
8. Speaking before groups usually requires extra effort. Stage fright may never disappear completely, but it can be controlled

X. SELF-DEVELOPMENT

1. Every employee is responsible for his own self-development.
2. Toastmaster and toastmistress clubs offer opportunities to improve skills in oral communications.
3. Planning for one's own self-development is of vital importance. Supervisors know their own strengths and limitations better than anyone else.
4. Many opportunities are open to aid the supervisor in his developmental efforts, including job assignments; training opportunities, both governmental and non-governmental -- to include universities and professional conferences and seminars.
5. Programmed instruction offers a means of studying at one's own rate.
6. Where difficulties may arise from a supervisor's being away from his work for training, he may participate in televised home study or correspondence courses to meet his self-development needs.

XI. TEACHING AND TRAINING

A. The Teaching Process

Teaching is encouraging and guiding the learning activities of students toward established goals. In most cases this process consists in five steps: preparation, presentation, summarization, evaluation, and application.

1. Preparation

   Preparation is twofold in nature; that of the supervisor and the employee.

   Preparation by the supervisor is absolutely essential to success. He must know what, when, where, how, and whom he will teach. Some of the factors that should be considered are:

   (1) The objectives   (5) Employee interest
   (2) The materials needed   (6) Training aids
   (3) The methods to be used   (7) Evaluation
   (4) Employee participation   (8) Summarization

   Employee preparation consists in preparing the employee to receive the material. Probably the most important single factor in the preparation of the employee is arousing and maintaining his interest. He must know the objectives of the training, why he is there, how the material can be used, and its importance to him.

2. Presentation

   In presentation, have a carefully designed plan and follow it. The plan should be accurate and complete, yet flexible enough to meet situations as they arise. The method of presentation will be determined by the particular situation and objectives.

3. Summary

   A summary should be made at the end of every training unit and program. In addition, there may be internal summaries depending on the nature of the material being taught. The important thing is that the trainee must always be able to understand how each part of the new material relates to the whole.

4. Application

   The supervisor must arrange work so the employee will be given a chance to apply new knowledge or skills while the material is still clear in his mind and interest is high. The trainee does not really know whether he has learned the material until he has been given a chance to apply it. If the material is not applied, it loses most of its value.

5. Evaluation

   The purpose of all training is to promote learning. To determine whether the training has been a success or failure, the supervisor must evaluate this learning.

   In the broadest sense evaluation includes all the devices, methods, skills, and techniques used by the supervisor to keep himself and the employees informed as to their progress toward the objectives they are pursuing. The extent to which the employee has mastered the knowledge, skills, and abilities, or changed his attitudes, as determined by the program objectives, is the extent to which instruction has succeeded or failed.

   Evaluation should not be confined to the end of the lesson, day, or program but should be used continuously. We shall note later the way this relates to the rest of the teaching process.

B. Teaching Methods

   A teaching method is a pattern of identifiable student and instructor activity used in presenting training material.

   All supervisors are faced with the problem of deciding which method should be used at a given time.

1. Lecture
   The lecture is direct oral presentation of material by the supervisor. The present trend is to place less emphasis on the trainer's activity and more on that of the trainee.
2. Discussion
   Teaching by discussion or conference involves using questions and other techniques to arouse interest and focus attention upon certain areas, and by doing so creating a learning situation. This can be one of the most valuable methods because it gives the employees an opportunity to express their ideas and pool their knowledge.
3. Demonstration
   The demonstration is used to teach how something works or how to do something. It can be used to show a principle or what the results of a series of actions will be. A well-staged demonstration is particularly effective because it shows proper methods of performance in a realistic manner.
4. Performance
   Performance is one of the most fundamental of all learning techniques or teaching methods. The trainee may be able to tell how a specific operation should be performed but he cannot be sure he knows how to perform the operation until he has done so.

As with all methods, there are certain advantages and disadvantages to each method.

5. Which Method to Use
   Moreover, there are other methods and techniques of teaching. It is difficult to use any method without other methods entering into it. In any learning situation a combination of methods is usually more effective than any one method alone.

Finally, evaluation must be integrated into the other aspects of the teaching-learning process.
It must be used in the motivation of the trainees; it must be used to assist in developing understanding during the training; and it must be related to employee application of the results of training.
This is distinctly the role of the supervisor.

———

ANSWER SHEET

TEST NO. _____ PART _____ TITLE OF POSITION_____

(AS GIVEN IN EXAMINATION ANNOUNCEMENT - INCLUDE OPTION. IF ANY)

PLACE OF EXAMINATION _____ DATE_____

(CITY OR TOWN)   (STATE)

RATING

USE THE SPECIAL PENCIL.   MAKE GLOSSY BLACK MARKS.

Make only ONE mark for each answer.   Additional and stray marks may be
counted as mistakes.   In making corrections, erase errors COMPLETELY.

1–25, 26–50, 51–75, 76–100, 101–125 (columns with answer bubbles A B C D E)

ANSWER SHEET

USE THE SPECIAL PENCIL. MAKE GLOSSY BLACK MARKS.

Columns of answer bubbles labeled A B C D E for questions 1 through 125.

1–25, 26–50, 51–75, 76–100, 101–125 (top block 1–10, 26–35, 51–60, 76–85, 101–110)

Make only ONE mark for each answer. Additional and stray marks may be counted as mistakes. In making corrections, erase errors COMPLETELY.

Questions 11–25, 36–50, 61–75, 86–100, 111–125